Second Edition

INTRODUCTION TO PERFORMANCE

Beginning the Creative Process of the Actor

Sarah Barker

Peter Harrigan

KENDALL/HUNT PUBLISHING COMPANY
4050 Westmark Drive Dubuque, Iowa 52002

Cover: Courtesy of Susan Stein O'Connell

Acknowledgements: Special thanks to Candice Brown, Maryellen Rowlett and the intrepid Linda Kaiserman.

Printed in the United States of America
10 9 8 7 6 5 4 3 2 1

CONTENTS

ACKNOWLEDGEMENTS

This edition of Introduction to Performance reflects the support and work of many individuals we would like to acknowledge. We are indebted to Candice Brown for the hours and hours she put in to collate and record the writing of the original workbook. Many thanks to Lynda Kaiserman for her un-flagging efforts in organizing the editions for this version. We wish to acknowledge Rachel Resinski's contribution of play review questions and Ellen Seeling's contribution of the rendering of a procenium theatre. Dr. Kathy George and Ann Marie Costa made invaluable suggestions for the shaping of this final version. Betty Tarantino has kept us sensible and succinct. Finally thanks to all of the teachers who have used this book helping us to refine it to this final form.

CHAPTER I

THE RICH GIFTS OF THE THEATRE

"To superimpose an imaginary reality upon actual reality is a tendency shared by all living beings—whether men or animals. What's the cause of it? Does the reason for it lie in the desire to live imaginatively a story which could not be lived if this story were true? One has all kinds of courage in imaginary situations. It is pleasant to play with the notion of fear when there is no real cause for fear. This desire for 'acting' comes perhaps from the urge to get a full grasp of real life and its problems through an artificial recreation of life, something which is really 'filtered' life, or life at one remove. This is something in which attitudes and behaviour are more clearly outlined and lucidity is not blinded by the urgency of decision. It is therefore a training ground for virtual actions which can be beneficial in cases of incapacity to act; it is a school of energy, a place where one recharges one's batteries."[1]
–Jean-Louis Barrault

Theatre at its best draws the spectator, the audience, into the power and immediacy of the actions on stage. It presents dramatic situations with fundamental differences from our own situation, but somehow creates strong connections between these real and fictive worlds. An audience member leaves the successful performance somehow changed, transformed in the way in which he views or experiences the world. If a person who visits the theatre only for the few hours of the performance—a stranger to the weeks and months of preparation—can be so moved or changed, think of the growth the cast and crew of the production experiences!

The production that the audience sees is a result of the collaborations of many diverse theatre artists. The physical production (scenery, lighting, costumes) is evolved over a period of many months to provide the clearest manifestation of the world of the play. The designers work with the director to vividly realize the action and meaning of the play in visual terms. They draw on talents as diverse as carpentry, graphic arts, historical research and computer science to create the imaginary world which the actors will inhabit.

Using both technical skill and well developed personal resources, the actors (this term refers to both male and female players) jump into the imaginary world of the play; they give three-dimensional life to the people who inhabit the world that the playwright has created in words.

"The whole history of the theatre shows us that it has its source in imitation, which of course is not the lifeless copying of nature, but the recreating of life through artificial means."[2] –Jean-Louis Barrault

1. Jean-Louis Barrault, ''How Drama is Born Within Us,'' in *The Making of Theatre,* ed. Robert W. Corrigan (Glenview, Ill.: Scott, Foresman, and Company, 1981), p. 2–3.
2. Ibid, p. 3.

When a person chooses to be an actor she or he is already endowed with natural human attributes learned in everyday interpersonal communication, as well as the qualities of imitation and role playing everyone possesses as a child. The actor builds on these resources, and channels them toward the specific actions and traits of the character as depicted by the playwright. The text has given the actor a clear structure within which to improvise, finding a personal method of using body, voice, imagination, and personal history, to fully serve the needs of the script and communicate its message to others.

The actor's training is highly focused and disciplined. Most traditional training programs require three or four years work, but the development of the actor is truly ongoing. Experience onstage and in life continually contributes to one's pool of resources. This comprehensive education prepares the actor for the challenges of many types of roles, each of which can be approached with a finely honed craft.

"Actors and actresses are in themselves fabulous beings and therefore qualified to express that which print can never adequately convey."[3] –Robert E. Sherwood

While show business success is sometimes a result of many factors outside the realm of craft or talent (the secretary discovered in the sandwich bar at MGM studios), the professional theatre artist, technician or performer, is a well trained, committed creative artist.

The study you are about to embark upon will provide the rudimentary skills with which aspiring actors must begin their journey. You will find that these skills are not exclusively useful to professional actors but will also enrich your interpersonal skills in everyday life and non-theatrical endeavors. Formal presentations are part of most vocations: the physical and vocal clarity you will learn in your study of acting will give you a competitive edge in the job market. By fully committing to the exercises and explorations in Introduction to Performance you will gain insight and sensitivity toward yourself and others. You will learn to appreciate and strengthen self-image, self-confidence and joyful self-expression. You will feel more able to express yourself to a group without heavy handed self-criticism and self-consciousness. You will be able to make more meaningful connections with others. In turn, your personal discoveries will illuminate your ability to act. Uta Hagen, master teacher of acting, puts it succinctly: *"First, you must learn to know who you are. You must find your own sense of identity, enlarge this sense of self, and learn to see how that knowledge can be put to use in the characters you will portray on stage."*[4]

3. Robert E. Sherwood, "The Dwelling Place of Wonder," in *The Making of Theatre,* ed. Robert W. Corrigan (Glenview, Ill.: Scott, Foresman, and Company, 1981), p. 13.
4. Uta Hagen, *Respect for Acting* (New York: Macmillan Publishing Co., Inc., 1973), p. 22.

CHAPTER II

BEGINNINGS

Good acting requires two very basic human skills that must be in place before the kind of training described in this text can begin: discipline and trust. Think of discipline as a gift you give to yourself and others. Your ability to arrive in class on time, dressed in clothing that is appropriate to the day's activities, and freed from the burdens of the rest of your day (at least for the period of time in which you are in class) will enable you to perform your role more successfully. The business of theatre—as well as any other field you plan to enter in your future—requires full commitment to attain a competitive edge: let your dedication begin today!

Trust is a more delicate matter, because it not only involves our feelings for ourselves, but also our sensitivity to the needs of others. In order for creative work to flower, all individuals must feel safe and free of scrutiny. If an ensemble—a group that has a common identity and mutual goal—can be formed within your classroom, everyone will feel freer to do both compelling and unsuccessful work in an atmosphere that will not single them out for either. A trusting environment is one in which it is fine to explore, experiment, and even to *fail* when first trying a new skill or task. Classroom work very *gradually* creates foundations for polished performances. By creating a supportive atmosphere, you will insure the comfort and safety of everyone in your class as you begin this journey together. The exercises included in this chapter are guidelines that your instructor may choose to use in order to break down personal barriers, and create a feeling of unity in the group.

Exercise 1: The Name Game

Sit in a circle, and designate a leader—this person may not necessarily be the teacher. The leader will say his or her first name, and then make a hand or body gesture that signifies him (for instance a peace sign, a Bronx cheer, or an ear tug). The person to the leader's left will in turn say his own name and create his own gesture, and then repeat those of the leader. The third person will state his name and choose a gesture, and then repeat those of the first and second. This progression will continue around the circle until the leader is called upon again to repeat *all* names and gestures, beginning and ending with his own. Names are important—they are one of the first basic tools that distinguish us as individuals.

Exercise 2: Coloring

Draw on this page the feelings you have as you begin this course. What you draw may express your current inner state, your recent accomplishments, or your long term goals. Your picture can be very realistic or very abstract. Your skill as an artist (or lack thereof) is not an issue here, just your honest self expression.

Exercise 3: Final Reflections

At the end of the semester draw a new picture of your inner state, accomplishments, growth and future goals. Compare it to the picture on page 5.

Exercise 4: Self Definition with Contact

Form a circle, standing up, and choose a new leader. The leader must walk around the inside of the circle and greet each person he encounters separately. The leader will say, I am Mary (substitute your name), You are John (substitute the name of each individual as you encounter them), and make some kind of physical contact (handshake, hug, or grasping of the hands, arms, or shoulders are a few suggestions). Try to make eye contact. If you can make a basic connection with another person (at this point a relative stranger), you have achieved a giant step toward honest communication with others on stage.

How did it feel to make contact? Scary? Exhilarating? How did it feel when others tried to contact you? Did you feel open to their attempts? Write your feelings about this experience below. Think about the physical and emotional feelings you experienced.

_____

_____

_____

_____

_____

Exercise 5: Photographic Memory

Bring in two photographs of you—one that expresses how you currently see yourself—and another which for some reason (different haircut, sun tan, outrageous clothing) looks like someone else. Share these photographs with your class, and discuss the context of each.

Exercise 6: Observations

Sit indian-style across from a partner, and carefully study their physical appearance, just as they are studying yours. Agree on a moment where you will both turn your backs to the other, and _alter_ four tangible things about yourself (remove jewelry, button up shirt, untie shoe). When you are both ready, face each other and try to determine what your partner has altered. When you have exhausted all of the possibilities, try the exercise with numerous other partners.

Exercise 7: Line Up!

Gather with your classmates and, with your eyes closed, arrange yourselves according to _height_ (with the tallest at one end, and the slightest at the other). Next, line yourselves according to _size of hands_. Next, try _size of feet_.

Exercise 8: I thought I was going to die!

Prepare and then present to the class, in the form of an improvised monologue, the story of one of your most embarrassing moments. Try to keep the story to five minutes in length, but be sure to cover all of the points that made it uniquely horrifying! Use the space below to create an outline.

_____

_____

_____

_____

How did you feel, up in front of the class, with the attention focused on you? Be as honest as possible—this will make great reading at the end of the course!

_____

_____

_____

_____

_____

Be proud of yourself—these exercises, and those that your instructor will supplement with involve taking risks. But the knowledge you will gain of yourself, and the trust, compassion, and friendship you will receive from your classmates will make it easier to stand up and fully participate next time.

CHAPTER III

THE ACTOR'S INSTRUMENT

The actor is a creative artist. He learns to play the score written by the playwright using the scale of human emotions and expression. The actor's medium, like the painter's acrylics, or the musician's violin, is *himself:* his body, his voice and his imagination.

The actor must explore, stretch and exercise his body, voice and imagination in order to expand his range of playing, and to gain precision and daring in the art of acting. In the theatre, the audience knows what a character feels and thinks only through the way in which the actor uses his movements and his voice. What the actor imagines is revealed in the nuances of gesture and shifts in vocal expression.

The mark of a professional actor is a well trained body and voice which spontaneously respond to his creative impulses. It takes many years to develop a strong physical and vocal technique. In the beginning study of acting you can concern yourself with fundamentals of movement, breathing and sounding that will give greater freedom in expressing thoughts and emotions. You will discover the powerful relationship between body and emotion: when changing movements your emotions are affected; when your emotional currents change it affects the body and voice. Through simple warm-up exercises and movement explorations you can strengthen the link between body and voice, and also thoughts and emotions. By focusing on the FIVE fundamental skills: Relaxation, Improved Kinesthetic Awareness, Vocal Freedom, Physical and Vocal Expressivity, Physical Characterization you will improve the ability to participate effectively in acting exercises, as well as insure that you are in the optimum state of ease and availability needed to perform as an actor.

You should begin all of your work sessions with a warm-up. Ordinarily, you bring the emotional, mental baggage of your life with you to class or rehearsal. If you're having a difficult time with classes you may come to acting class worried or in a bad mood. You may be trying to solve all of the problems you've encountered in the week by keeping a running list of them in your head. Or perhaps you just feel tired or lazy. The warm-up is your opportunity to rid yourself of these normal burdens, at least temporarily, so you can enter a creative, playful state. Warm-ups should be structured to help you achieve a centered state: relaxed, breathing freely, with a sense of freedom and ease about yourself.

Relaxation

Constantin Stanislavski, the great director and acting teacher says of physical tension,

"Among the nervous people of our generation this muscular tensity is inescapable. To destroy it completely is impossible, but we must struggle with it incessantly. Our method consists of developing a sort of control; an observer, as it were. This observer must, under all circumstances, see that at no point

9

shall there be an extra amount of contraction. This process of self-observation and removal of unnecessary tenseness should be developed to the point where it becomes a subconscious, mechanical habit. Nor is that sufficient. It must be a normal habit and a natural necessity, not only during the quieter parts of your role, but especially at times of the greatest nervous and physical lift.[1] He goes on to say that one can learn to *constantly* relax.

When you are in a state of total relaxation your body is limp, as in sleeping. This is not the state of relaxation that enhances your acting ability. You must learn to be as relaxed and energized as possible in a standing and moving state. However, a few experiences of total relaxation can make you more aware and familiar with how to release excess muscular tension whenever you need to.

Improving Kinesthetic Awareness

The perception of the position and movement of your muscles and joints is kinesthetic awareness.

Most of us are quite unaware of this sense in daily activity, only noticing our physical body if we experience pain or sudden relief from discomfort. By heightening kinesthetic awareness, you can improve your presentation of yourself and control over your movement. You will know when your posture and gestures are projecting the impression that you desire. You will accurately judge when you are using too much effort, or one part of your body is excessively tense. You will quickly realize if you have restricted your breathing, or if you are straining your voice. In order to train your kinesthetic awareness, check yourself several times a day simply to notice how you are using your body, and if there are sensations you have been ignoring.

Exercise 1: Kinesthetic Awareness

Write a description of what you notice during one of those moments of listening to your body. Include notes on the following:

1. What parts of your body are you aware of?
2. Where do you feel tension or pressure?
3. Where in your body is your breath moving?
4. What is your mental state? What kind of thinking are you doing?
5. What position are you holding your spine in?

_____

_____

_____

_____

_____

_____

_____

_____

_____

_____

1. Constantin Stanislavski, "Relaxation of Muscles," in *An Actor Prepares* (Theatre Arts Books, 1969). p. 93.

_____

_____

_____

_____

Whenever you're participating in physical activities in acting class—whether it's warm-ups, improvisations, scene work—take stock of your body using your kinesthetic sense. When you discover you are using too much tension and effort, use your mind to direct the tension to release: direct your body to work with less effort.

Exercise 2: Constructive Rest Position

Lie on the floor on your back. Notice any parts of your body you are holding with tension and let them go. Think of letting the floor hold you. Keep your feet flat on the floor at a distance of approximately eighteen inches apart and your knees bent up toward the ceiling. Let your legs fall in against each other so that the knees touch, supporting each other as do two cards in a house of cards. This position allows you to completely release the muscles of the legs. The small of the back can be released flat against the floor. Place your arms by your sides, with hands on your abdomen. Make sure that your head is aligned with the center-line of your body, and not tipped to one side or the other. Face directly toward the ceiling without lifting your chin or jamming your chin into your neck. Leave a nice easy curve in the back of your neck.

This position enables the body to conserve maximum energy. It is stressless, requiring minimal muscular holding. Several minutes in this position with proper respiration can renew the body almost as well as sleep.

When you lie relaxed on your back and spread your weight evenly, you rely on the support of the ground, and feel no need to lift or hold any part of your body.

Make a detailed journal entry in which you examine your sense of your physical self. Where are you aware of physical tension in your body? When your body is aligned well as you lie on the floor do you feel crooked? Where are you aware of your breath moving in your body? How do you picture your size, your appearance, your grace? What part of you is most expressive?

_____

_____

_____

_____

_____

_____

_____

_____

Choose a partner and share your perceptions.

Exercise 3: Contraction-Release

This exercise is good to do if you are tired and have no time to take a nap.

The principle involved in this exercise is to work a muscle group very hard, then let go. This is achieved by consciously letting the muscles you have just worked go limp so that there is a feeling of heaviness and inertia. The following relaxation exercise should be learned and practiced regularly as part of your daily exercise program. Like any skill, the more you work at it, the more successful you will be.

Read the exercise through once or twice until you understand what you will be doing.

Begin in the constructive rest position. Then let your legs slide straight out on the floor, leaving your back relaxed on the floor. Tense your right leg, including toes, ankle, knee, and thigh as hard as you can. Hold this tension for a few seconds, then go limp. Do not move the right leg after it has become limp and heavy. Now try the left leg. Tense the toes, knee, and thigh. Hold the tension, then release it, letting the entire leg get heavy and limp. Concentrate on what you are doing so that you do not move either leg as you continue to work. Tense both buttocks, then release. Tense the stomach muscles and the back muscles and chest muscles as hard as you can, then release. Tense your right arm, fingers, forearm, upper arm. Release the tension. Repeat, using your left arm and taking care not to move the right arm. Keeping both arms still, tense your shoulders as hard as you can. Hold the tension, then release. Repeat using neck muscles. Now tighten your facial muscles around the eyes, nose, mouth, and forehead. Let go, checking each area to make sure there is no residual tension.

Allow a large breath to fill your torso; release it very slowly and imagine that as the breath leaves your body, all of the tension leaves your body. Feel all the tension and tightness melt from your body. You should feel completely loose, heavy and still, totally at peace. Stay this way for several minutes. End the exercise by putting your arms over your head on the floor, and stretching your whole body as you would to wake yourself up in the morning. Enjoy feeling all of your muscles slowly wake up.

To get up without adding new unnecessary tension to your body, use the following procedure:

Fold your knees up over your body then drop them to one side or the other. Let your upper body roll effortlessly toward the side your knees have dropped to. Slowly push yourself up to sitting with your arms, but leave your head hanging heavily from your neck. It takes some practice to leave your head hanging, so get someone to watch you do this movement: make sure you leave your neck released. Next, roll over onto your hands and knees still leaving your head hanging. Tuck your toes under your feet and push yourself easily onto your feet. You will be in a squatting position. Then let your hips float up leaving your knees slightly bent. You will be bent over at the hips with your arms and head hanging down toward the floor. To complete standing you will roll up your spine.

Exercise 4: Roll Up the Spine

Focus your attention on your tailbone and begin at that point to stack the vertebra one on top of the other. Imagine stacking them as you would building blocks, only imagine leaving a little space in between the blocks. Do not use your stomach muscles; continue to release them so that they are soft and easy. Continue to breath easily. Let your knees gradually straighten as your body becomes more and more upright. Leave your head hanging forward until the last moment. Then build up the separate vertebrae of the neck. Imagine your head floating up on top of your spine. If you get dizzy or slightly light-headed simply drop your head forward again until you have adjusted to being in the standing position. You can roll back down your spine in the same manner and then back up.

Once you are standing you will probably feel more balanced and that less effort is required to stand. This is possible because you have let go of unnecessary gripping, pushing and tightening by rolling up and down your spine. The more you practice it, the more you will become familiar with this easy balance of the parts of the body, one on top of the other.

Vocal Freedom

It is as important to have freedom and ease in your vocal apparatus as it is to have a free and relaxed body. This kind of freedom starts with freeing your breathing so that your speaking voice is clear and strong without excess effort. The key to freeing your breath is to release the unnecessary tension in your torso, belly and spine. You have already learned some exercises that generally affect these areas of habitual tension: deep relaxation and rolling up the spine. Now you can focus a little more on releasing your belly and allowing breathing that is more full than you have experienced before.

The actor needs to have a strong breathing mechanism and expressive voice without over-controlling or speaking in a false or sing-song manner. Most people find that if they can let go of extra vocal tension they have much more breath capacity and vocal power without even trying for more.

Many people constrict the breath into the upper part of the chest, holding the belly flat or tight. In acting training it has become clear that the imagination and emotions are most available with a released and relaxed belly, and a full breath that is breathed in the ribs, the back, and the belly. So get used to letting your stomach go in an acting class. Your vanity may suffer slightly but your health will benefit, and your acting ability will improve. Yes, just by learning to leave your belly muscles free to breath fully and easily your acting will improve.

Exercise 5: Imaging Sounds

Write about what you have experienced in breathing this way. Even if you were not very successful, write about it.

_____

_____

_____

_____

_____

_____

_____

_____

Connecting Sound To Your Center

Your solar plexus is located directly below your sternum. It is a ganglion of nerves knit into your diaphragm which is intimately connected with your emotions and thoughts. Your objective in the following exercise is to release any tension around your solar plexus and to allow your breath and then your sound to be connected with your solar plexus. This will allow your voice to express what you are feeling very clearly to an audience.

Of course, your breath actually moves in and out of your lungs. However, for the purposes of this exercise, imagine your breath moving into your whole torso, all the way down to your hip sockets. This encourages many of the muscles in your torso to relax and move with the flow of your breath.

Lie down in constructive rest position. Focus your attention first on letting your back release into the floor. Then focus on letting your breathing move your belly up when you allow breath in, and then letting your belly fall inward as your breath releases from your body. Imagine that a little stone drops onto your belly each time you finish inhaling. Let the imaginary stone gently press your breath out of your body. It is as if your breath falls out of your body effortlessly. Let the breath naturally flow back into your body without sucking or pulling it in. With each release of breath imagine the stone falling and the breath falling out. As you continue to allow the breath to rise and fall in your belly begin to focus on the breath also moving into your back. Your back will expand with the inward flow, and release toward the floor as the breath falls out. Work with yourself to allow the breath to be effortless, full, and relaxed.

Next, imagine that there is a pool in your belly. It's like a pool of water—only the liquid is *vibration*. Every time your breath drops out of your body it takes a little of the vibration with it. As your breath falls out of your body it leaves as pure vibration. It will be like a tiny touch of sound released on your breath. At first it is difficult to let the sound happen without adding effort to the sound. Your objective is to *allow* the sound rather than making it. It should be effortless and of pure vibration (rather than breathy). It will sound like a small "huh" riding on the breath.

See if you can allow changes in your sound (this is the opposite of deliberately producing changes in your sound to indicate change in your thought).

Try this experiment: Imagine you are laying on a tropical beach being warmed by the sun. Imagine that you breath that image into your body and into your belly. Then let vibration or sound carry the image out of you. Your sound might change, perhaps to an "oooo," perhaps to an "aaahhh."

Imagine putting your hand into icy water. Breath in the image. Sigh it out with the vibration. How does the sound change?

Try some other images. Notice how they effect the vibration without you adding any effort.

Exercise 6: Imaging Sounds

Write about what you have experienced in breathing and making sound this way. Even if you were not very successful, write about it.

_____

_____

_____

_____

_____

_____

_____

_____

_____

Physical and Vocal Expressivity

Another important aspect of training yourself is to gain freedom, flexibility and variety in your physical and vocal expression. To explore the many possibilities for moving and sounding that you possess, you need to first warm-up your joints and muscles for more vigorous activity.

The following exercises are designed to give you many opportunities to move in unfamiliar and imaginative ways. The more playful you become with your movement and sound, the easier it will be to express yourself fully in acting improvisations, scene rehearsals, and even in life.

Exercise 7: Loosening Joints

1. *Head:* Keeping the shoulders still, circle the head around slowly, first to one side, then the other. If neck muscles are sore or very tense, massage the sore muscles with your hands.
2. *Shoulders:* Circle one shoulder, then the other, going around both forward and backward. Work both shoulders at the same time, or sequentially. Keep fingers and wrists relaxed, torso lengthened.
3. *Torso:* With arms relaxed at sides and head in line with body, circle the torso from the waist, first to one side, then to the other. Work with knees bent. Putting your hands on your hips can help you isolate your upper torso from your hips and keep your balance.
4. *Legs:* Put your hands on your knees and circle the knees forward, to the side, back and to the other side in a circle. This exercise uses your hip joints, knees, ankles and feet.

Exercise 8: Shaking

Shake each part of your body very loosely and effortlessly. Try to get each part to shake without tensing any other part, almost as if another force were doing the shaking for you. Start with your hands, move the shaking up your arms, shake your shoulders, across your back. Shake down your spine, shake one leg and then the other. Then shake your face and let sound shake out of your mouth. Finally shake your whole self: don't be afraid to make some crazy shaking noises!

Exercise 9: Slow Motion

Walk around the room at normal speed. Now start to slow the walk down. Become slower and slower until you are moving with full gestures in slow motion. Take note of how the muscles are working. Eliminate any extraneous motions that are not a part of a real walk.

Sit down and stand up from a chair. Then repeat it in slow motion. Don't add any unnecessary movements. Notice how your upper body counter-balances your hips in order to maintain control.

Pretend that you are doing an everyday activity like making a sandwich or folding clothes. Do it without real props and do it as if you are in a hurry. Now maintain the same urgency but do the activity in slow motion.

Exercise 10: Stretching and Justifying

Stretch your body in any way that you like. Include every part of you in the stretches you try. Stretch your face, tongue, feet, hands, everything.

During the stretching freeze suddenly. Allow yourself to freeze in whatever strange stretching motion you are in. NOW, justify the position you are in by thinking of an action or activity that would call for you to be in that position. For example if you are bending over with one of your arms reaching between your legs, maybe you are about to shoe a horse and you are going to bring the hoof between your legs. Go on with the activity and complete it. Then resume stretching, and find other poses to justify.

Exercise 11: Throwing Sound

Start shaking out one hand and arm. Shake it more and more vigorously and let it rise up in front of your body until you can throw the shaking away with a shout of sound.
Throw the other hand and arm away, throwing a sound with it. Throw the shaking out through a leg, through the other leg, through your back and through your belly. Always throw sound with it. Then throw the shaking away through your whole body. It will be like an explosion.

Exercise 12: Follow the Leader

Form a line with all the people in your group. The person at the front is the leader. The leader's objective is to take the group through several unusual repetitive movement patterns. There should always be accompanying sound that has a similar quality to the movement, i.e. short hopping movements create short sharp sounds.

Exercise 13: Obstacle Course

Fill the room with objects; chairs, benches, ladders, a hat, a pile of notebooks, a piece of chalk. Lay them out on the floor to make an obstacle course. Move through the obstacle course, moving around, over and through the obstacles in as many unusual ways as you can think of. Watch the people go before you; find ways that are new and different from their ways.

After you have run the course once, have someone in the group call freeze as you are going through the course. Try to stop in whatever movement you are doing without wobbling or loosing your balance.

Exercise 14: Sound Mirror

Pick a partner. Partner number one is the sounder. When he makes a sound, partner number two moves according to the quality of the sound. Partner number one can try to make sounds that will make his partner move in unusual and varied ways. See what happens when you make very quiet sound, very loud sound, sudden sound, repetitive sounds. After you have moved all the way across the room, switch partners so that partner number two is the sounder.

Physical Characterization

The way in which you use your body as you move about on the stage tells the audience what kind of person your character is. By exploring changes in your physical carriage you will discover how to effect the impression you make on others as well as the way you feel psychologically about yourself.

Exercise 15: Changing Your Movement

As you mill about the room at a moderate walking pace, carry your body in the different ways listed below. Notice how the rest of your body needs to adjust to the change in one body part. Notice how the change influences the way you feel about yourself and the thoughts that occur to you. After you try each change, return to a relaxed natural walk before you make a new change. After you have finished the exercise, record a short description of how you felt and how you thought with each body change. You may even get an image of being somebody very specific such as a cowboy, or a large fat white-haired nanny, a shy little girl, a favorite uncle of yours, a childhood neighbor or a friend. Include any such images in your notes.

slump your chest _____

_____

_____

take baby steps _____

_____

_____

float your arms around your body _____

_____

_____

tuck your chin in _____

_____

_____

let your hips float back behind you _____

_____

_____

make your belly huge and bulging forward _____

_____

_____

keep your hands moving quickly in fidgety movements _____

_____

_____

fill lots of space with your legs _____

_____

_____

Make up some physical changes of your own. If you observe the people around you in restaurants, on the bus, walking to class, and in other places you will discover many unusual ways in which normal people carry themselves.

Exercise 16: Playing With Centers

Another way to think about changing the way your character moves is to find the physical center. The four main centers are the head, chest, belly, and pelvis. By experimenting you can also create other centers such as knees or shoulders or nose. Once you choose a center, move as if that part pushes or pulls your body around the room. React to your classmates and execute actions with the center leading you.

Explore each of the four centers, and record your feelings and thoughts. What kind of person leads with the head, or the chest, or the pelvis? Make note of one person you have observed using each center. Describe the kind of character you concluded the person was from the way the person moved.

head _____

_____

_____

the person I observed was _____

_____

_____

chest _____

_____

the person I observed was _____

_____

_____

belly _____

_____

the person I observed was _____

_____

_____

pelvis _____

_____

_____

the person I observed was _____

_____

_____

write about one other center _____

_____

_____

the person I observed was _____

_____

_____

Rehearsals

When you begin rehearsing projects or scenes for acting class, use this kind of movement play to open yourself up to the most interpretations possible for a scene. Your physical experience can inspire all sorts of ideas that you would never think of if you just sat in a chair and tried to come up with ''good ideas'' for your scene work.

Find out what happens to a scene if you do the dialogue while you are trying to move through an obstacle course, or chasing your partner through the obstacle course, or whispering the scene to each other in the dark. You'll be able to come up with many more physical ways to rehearse a scene if you approach it with the objective to be playful and explore.

Explore physical choices for your character paying attention to how the choices make you think and feel. See how the playing of your scene is affected by using one of the four centers.

CHAPTER IV

THE ACTOR'S BASIC SKILLS

The raw materials for the art of acting are: your five senses, your memory, emotions, and imagination.

You use your imagination to shape the other basic elements into a dramatic performance by playing actions that will achieve objectives that you choose.

In this chapter you will begin observing the most basic experiences of your five senses, and graduate to conditioning forces and finally to emotional experiences. Then you will begin to look at how to shape a performance by choosing actions, objectives, obstacles and subtext for the character.

The Five Senses

In order to train yourself and study the five senses or emotion all you need to do is pay more attention to yourself and what happens to you in every day life. Uta Hagen says that if someone simply stays alert that person will notice that no matter how normal one's life is, it is filled with important moments and special events. By observing your own reactions to specific events you can remember them, and reproduce them when you need them in an improvisation or a scene. As you do the following written exercises and exercises in class you will become more and more successful at describing and finally believably reproducing sense experiences.

Notice how you react physically to each of the five senses. Take them one at a time and observe your experience in detail, then write down on the following pages the descriptions of your experience. For example, if someone were to take a bite of a lemon they might describe their reactions as follows: "Held my breath, scrunched my face, my jaws tensed, the back of my neck tightened, I heard a roaring in my ears, then I started to salivate a lot and my stomach began to turn, I saw yellow and then I shook my head, it was a kind of excited energy running through my body."

The next step, once you have learned to observe your senses in detail, is to learn to use the five senses as tools in acting. First practice reacting again as you remember experiencing a particular sense. Second, exaggerate your reaction until your whole body learns to let each sense experience affect your whole body, that way when you're on stage the audience will see exactly how you're feeling. For example, think of tasting lemon again—your jaw might tense and your lips squeeze together. Exaggerate that by squeezing your shoulders and torso together and tensing your neck. Your whole body will be involved.

In an acting scene it's not likely you could use such an exaggerated response (unless in a comedy) but by exaggerating now you will find it easier to heighten your reaction subtly throughout your whole body just enough for the stage.

Finally, you need to learn to **ENDOW** stage props or objects with the qualities of real objects. Experiment with a simple object like a scarf and pretend that it has qualities it doesn't really have. For example, imagine that its been dropped in sewage and is dripping with smelly liquid; or maybe it shimmers like gold; or maybe it feels like cashmere; or perhaps you hear it rip as you pick it up. Pay attention to recreating the sense memory fully for yourself. If you can do it now, it will be a cinch in a scene. Try other objects and **ENDOW** them with other qualities.

Conditioning Forces

Often times in portraying a character there are **CONDITIONING FORCES** that affect your physical senses and change your physical state. The actions you are to recreate in a scene are affected by conditioning forces such as heat, cold, dark, needing to be quiet, feeling nausea, or being drunk, a headache, a broken arm, or sleepiness. This list is endless. You can build on the work you have done with the five senses to develop the ability to portray these conditions, and even to portray two or more at a time. Start with researching the affect these conditions have on you in real life situations. Notice how you move across a familiar room in the dark; across a strange room. When you are writing a paper how do the actions change when you are hot and sweaty; when you are icy cold; or when there isn't enough light? Exercise 3: Conditioning Forces will help you begin your research.

Sometimes you must play a scene in which several conditioning forces affect your work at one time. Make certain the first one becomes so well practiced that you do it almost without thinking about it, then *add* the second, work with it until it is also automatic, then the third, etc. Save the most difficult or the one that requires more attention to maintain, like nausea or drunkenness, for last.

Emotions

A personal study of your emotions can proceed in a similar manner to your five senses work. Begin by observing yourself during moments of high emotionality and record the following:

> What tensions, contractions do you feel in your muscles, and in what specific areas of the body?
>
> Do you change your posture, (drop your head, slump chest, make fists, etc.)?
>
> How does your breathing change?
>
> How do you feel inside your body?
>
> Do you have a sense of color, texture or motion change in your insides? For example: If you are angry you might feel your fists clench, your teeth grind, your neck and shoulders tense and your breath get heavier; also, you might feel internally a burning, or a rock-like compression in your belly, or a color of black-red brick might come to mind.

Turn to Exercise 4 to begin your exploration of emotional experience.

On the following page record your observations of the following emotional states in yourself. Give yourself at least a week to find yourself in these different emotional states. It is preferable for you to observe yourself in the moment of the experience but if absolutely necessary you can draw from your memory a past experience of a particular emotion.

Exercise 1: Sensory Reactions

Your own reaction to a bite of lemon could be similar or very different from the one above. Try it and record it below:

When I bit a lemon: _____

_____

_____

_____

_____

_____

_____

_____

When I smelled coffee: _____

_____

_____

_____

_____

_____

_____

_____

_____

When I step in some wet, smelly garbage: _____

_____

_____

_____

_____

_____

_____

_____

_____

When I saw the sky today: _____

_____

_____

_____

_____

_____

_____

_____

When I heard a siren: _____

_____

_____

_____

_____

_____

_____

_____

_____

Exercise 2: Remembering Sensory Reactions

Now pick your own experience of each of the five senses from your past, and describe it.

Sight: _____

_____

_____

_____

_____

Smell: _____

_____

_____

_____

_____

Touch: _____

_____

_____

_____

_____

Taste: _____

_____

_____

_____

_____

Sound: _____

_____

_____

_____

_____

Exercise 3: Conditioning Forces

Write about 5 different conditioning forces and their effect on you.

Exercise 4: Emotional Memories

Record your observations of the following emotional states in yourself.

Boredom: _____

_____

_____

_____

_____

_____

Sadness or Grief: _____

_____

_____

_____

_____

_____

_____

Anxious Anticipation: _____

_____

_____

_____

_____

_____

_____

Fear: _____

_____

_____

_____

_____

_____

_____

Joy: _____

_____

_____

_____

_____

_____

_____

_____

Hatred: _____

_____

_____

_____

_____

_____

_____

_____

_____

Record two other emotional states you have experienced. _____

_____

_____

_____

_____

_____

_____

_____

_____

_____

_____

_____

_____

Using Emotional Recall

Sometimes we are called on to portray emotional states that we do not experience very often. In such a case you can use an emotional memory to teach or remind yourself of all that you experienced in that high emotional state. Then when you are in the scene you can re-create that emotional state in response to the given circumstances of the play or scene.

Take the time to relax yourself, and then remember and write in detail of a real event in your past in which you experienced a strong emotion, i.e., anger, sadness, joy. Remember details that involve all five senses: the color of the room, the temperature, what the place where you were looked like, the smells, physical sensations, sounds.

Look for a "trigger object." In other words a trigger object is a specific detail, a color, a particular dress someone wore during the event, a table in the room, the memory of which brings the emotion back to you so that you experience it again. If you are successful, every time you think of the specific TRIGGER OBJECT it will reactivate the emotion. When you are playing a scene in which your belief in the given circumstances is not sufficient to evoke a particular emotion you can use your emotional recall. It is not intended that you use it in such a way that you suddenly remember your own experience while standing on stage playing a scene. Rather you can associate (or ENDOW) a stage property (for example, a letter from the character's long lost love) with your trigger object so that every time you see the stage prop it evokes the emotion associated with the trigger object. The final step is to use your imagination to create the stage prop as the character's trigger object for the emotional memory which should be remembered at that moment in the play. This is a lot of work to make one moment in a play work so it is always preferable to simply believe in the circumstances of the play to the extent that you are emotionally moved by the pretend situation. Emotional recall is really only necessary when nothing else works powerfully enough.

One caution: **Don't use an event that you are not healthily complete with. Pick something that happened at least two years ago and with which your feelings and thoughts are resolved in the present. This is a tool for acting and not a psychological tool for purging or healing a past emotional trauma.**

Action

While developing your expressiveness with the five senses and emotions will greatly facilitate your performing of a role it is most important to develop other skills that will shape or guide your performance with respect to the events of the story.

Acting is not about "being." An actor who tries to simulate being excited, being morose, being clumsy, or being drunk, no matter how skillfully he may perform the external shell, will give a hollow performance unless it springs from the action of the character and the action of the play. Similarly, an actor who concentrates on "feeling" afraid, angry, or sad, despite his technical proficiency, will deliver cold gestures separate from the action of the play. These states are not actable because they give the actor nothing to *do. Doing* or *action* is what draws the audience in—excites, amuses or moves them. More important, it gives the actor a hook into each scene of the play as it relates to the whole structure.

Action must first be separated from *activity*. Plays are filled with references to characters involved in activities—making phone calls, reading books, painting toenails, and the like. On a basic level, these bits of stage business fill the actor's time on stage, and give him a stronger sense of context (the genteel lady drops her clothing, then her maid picks it up). But in and of themselves, they don't create dramatic conflict. Choosing active verbs to describe what your character does with regard to the events of the play does create dramatic action and conflict on the stage. These active verbs are calls **ACTIONS.**

When attached to a larger *action,* the smaller activities become more effective: making a phone call *to urge* your parents not to come home early; reading a book *to avoid* contact with your soon-to-be-ex-spouse; painting your toenails *to irritate* your roommate with the smell of the polish. In everyday life, our actions are nearly always purposeful—we ''act'' to stop the policeman from ticketing our car, to persuade a customer that the dress fits her, and to convince our instructor that our tardiness was beyond our control. Your actions on stage, whether tied to physical activity or not, should seek to have this same sort of effect on your scene partner.

Stage action should always be considered *reciprocal.* Force is being exerted from both directions, even though one character may seem to dominate or even ''win'' the bout. In its most obvious form, action is a tug-of-war—both characters are moving or moved when the rope changes position. Sometimes conflict is as overt as a rope pull—but more often it is subtler. Perhaps the action of a character in a scene is to deceive or seduce. Though the author generally determines the outcome of a particular struggle, the actors decide, through the force of their actions, how desperate the battle becomes.

Action is one of the chief forces that comprises character. What a character says, and what others say about him is helpful in determining shades of personality, but the undeniable core lies in what the character DOES. He exists through his actions, particularly the things he does when under pressure. An actor can discover a great deal about the character by *doing* his **ACTIONS** in a committed manner in rehearsal.

Objectives

Just as important as the action itself, is the *reason* why the character feels compelled to pursue this course. Exploring character motivation involves careful study of the scene plus a bit of amateur psychology. OBJECTIVE is the term we will use for this element of ''why.'' An objective is a specific thing that a character wants or needs, that he can gain through **ACTION.** In *Agnes of God* by John Pielmeier, Dr. Livingstone wants to find out whether or not Agnes gave birth to (and subsequently murdered) a baby found in the convent. In *A Streetcar Named Desire* by Tennessee Williams, Blanche wants to escape from her past and create a life of pleasant illusion in New Orleans. In *The Glass Menagerie* by Tennessee Williams, Amanda wants to attract suitors for the painfully shy Laura. In each case the characters perform very specific actions in order to achieve their goals.

Objectives are most clearly expressed by using the phrase ''I want to'' followed by an *active* verb. Please avoid the verb ''to be'' at all costs; it tends to lead actors to descriptive words, rather than action-linked ones. These words turn back on themselves, rather than sending their force outward to change another character. Can you think of objectives you've had recently in your life? List several below, being careful to use strong active verbs:

_____

_____

_____

_____

_____

Obstacles

Most characters have an overriding desire that shapes their conduct throughout the play. This can be called a MAIN OBJECTIVE. And in each individual scene they have smaller goals—or IMMEDIATE OBJECTIVES—the accomplishment of which generally contributes to their overall want or need.

A character may not achieve his goal quickly—or ever—since objectives must involve the other character. As was previously discussed, plays come alive through conflict. Your objective must place demands on the other characters and bring you into conflict with them. You may find that your objective exists in direct opposition to your partner's. For instance, Stanley in *Streetcar* wants to maintain his hold on his domain, and his wife; Blanche's presence seems to undermine his attempts. In response, Stanley tries to humiliate Blanche and drive her away by exposing her past. Poor Blanche seems to have decreased chances of fulfilling her objective, since Stanley stands quite squarely in her way. Stanley is her OBSTACLE. Obstacles can be either physical or psychological, or some combination of both. Obstacles raise the stakes or add urgency to the struggle—and make for more excitement for both participants and viewers.

Take this opportunity to state your character's main and immediate objectives. Be sure to use the format established earlier in the chapter:

_____

_____

What is your character's obstacle (or obstacles) to achieving this goal?

_____

_____

Subtext

Sometimes a character pursues his objective obviously and directly throughout the course of the play. But more often than not, he must build to the pursuit of his goal gradually, and take indirect action. In Shakespeare's tragedy *Macbeth,* Macbeth and Lady Macbeth must slowly and carefully rid the kingdom of threats and successors to the throne, in order to avoid suspicion. The audience, however, is aware of their treachery, and is able to read into the seemingly innocent conversations they have with other characters. This duality—in which the actor makes the surface language convey an underlying meaning is called SUBTEXT. Subtext is what the line means to the character who says it, even though this may not be the literal meaning of the words. The audience sees what the "deceived" character misses, and therefore has a more meaningful experience of the play. The surface activity through which the subtext is presented carefully conceals it. Subtext helps engage the actor in strong exchanges, and work toward his goals in a less overt manner.

Find three lines in your scene which would support subtext. What do you think they mean?

_____

_____

_____

_____

_____

_____

All of this work prepares you to have at your command the raw materials needed in the art of acting. As a successful acting student you will finally be able to use your imagination to create an imagined reality of a scene. You will depend less on remembering how you experienced a sight or sound or an emotion and will instead play with the "magic if," that is when you can respond to any invented circumstances as if they were really happening to you. Enable your imagination by nurturing and sensitizing your five senses and your emotional life. You will construct your experience step by step and find your five senses alive with the stimuli of, for example, the imagined jungle you are in; adrenalin will actually pump through your body as you stalk the imagined dangerous and treacherous prey.

CHAPTER V

OPEN SCENES

In the previous chapter, you were introduced to the actor's basic skills. This chapter will give you a chance to employ some of these skills on a shorter text, before diving into script analysis work on a full-length play. These shorter scenes, called open scenes, are often devoid of specific content. They are made up of lines between characters that do not dictate a specific relationship or context, but may suggest different scenarios to individual actors. Let's take an example:

Actor A: Yes?
Actor B: No.
Actor A: Why?
Actor B: Because.
Actor A: When?
Actor B: Soon.

What particular circumstances might give meaning to these seemingly random lines? How many different objectives can you think of to pursue using this scene. What obstacles can be in your way and what actions can you take to overcome them? Here are a couple of the many possible interpretations:

—Both actors are travelling in a car—Actor A is a child pestering his parent to find out how far is it to their destination.

—Both actors are on a street corner. Actor A is a loan shark in search of payment. Actor B is his unprepared client.

Think of at least two more interpretations of this scene.

The remainder of this chapter is made up of nine longer open scenes for you to explore with a partner. Your instructor will be assigning one of these open scenes for you to work on with a partner. After you read the scene brainstorm with your partner and write down ideas about characters and objectives. Make sure your ideas are supported by the lines of the text. Perform the scene for your classmates in a rehearsed and memorized fashion and see if your classmates can tell the specific context and circumstances of your scene from your presentation. Be specific.

OPEN SCENE #1

A: Where have you been?
B: Out.
A: What did you do?
B: Nothing
A: Sure?
B: Oh yes, I'm sure.
A: I don't understand.
B: Of course you don't.
A: I want to understand.
B: Why do you care?
A: I don't know.
B: What's going on?
A: Not much.
B: How's your mom?
A: Fine. Fine. Fine.
B: So what are we talking about?

1. Where does the scene take place? _____

_____

2. What is the relationship between the characters? _____

_____

_____

_____

3. What is your character's objective? _____

_____

_____

_____

4. What obstacles stand in the way of achieving the objective? _____

_____

_____

5. What, if anything, does your character do to overcome these obstacles? _____

_____

_____

OPEN SCENE #2

A: Well?
B: Yes.
A: Yes?
B: I think so.
A: Unbelievable!
B: But we didn't actually speak.
A: What?
B: We didn't actually speak.
A: You are incredible.
B: But I know.
A: Hah!
B: She spoke.
A: HAH!
B: That's how I know.
A: Come back tomorrow
B: Please.
A: Go.

_____

1. Where does the scene take place? _____

_____

2. What is the relationship between the characters? _____

_____

_____

_____

3. What is your character's objective? _____

_____

_____

_____

4. What obstacles stand in the way of achieving the objective? _____

_____

_____

_____

5. What, if anything, does your character do to overcome these obstacles?_____

_____

_____

_____

OPEN SCENE #3

A: Oh, excuse me.
B: Oh, excuse me.
A: I'm sorry
B: It's okay. I'm sorry.
A: What?
B: Nothing.
A: Oh.
B: Hand me that, would you?
A: This?
B: Yeah.
A: It's not yours.
B: Hand it to me.
A: Well, alright.
B: Thank you.
A: Really, I didn't think . . .
B: Shsh.
A: Oh.
B: Sorry, What was that?
A: Nothing.
B: No.

1. Where does the scene take place? _____

_____

2. What is the relationship between the characters? _____

_____

_____

_____

_____

3. What is your character's objective? _____

_____

_____

4. What obstacles stand in the way of achieving the objective? _____

_____

_____

_____

5. What, if anything, does your character do to overcome these obstacles?_____

_____

_____

_____

OPEN SCENE #4

A: No, no, no, no, no.
B: Take it easy
A: How can you say that?
B: Listen this is no big deal.
A: No big deal.
B: I'm your friend, right?
A: Right.
B: I wouldn't mislead you.
A: I guess not.
B: You guess not. Now I'm hurt.
A: Well I didn't mean. . . .
B: No, no, no, no. You said ''guess.'' I know what you mean.
A: Oh, this is terrible.
B: What?
A: I'm miserable.
B: That's why I'm here. Let me help.

1. Where does the scene take place? _____

_____

_____

2. What is the relationship between the characters? _____

_____

_____

_____

_____

_____

3. What is your character's objective? _____

_____

_____

_____

_____

4. What obstacles stand in the way of achieving the objective? _____

_____

_____

_____

5. What, if anything, does your character do to overcome these obstacles?_____

_____

_____

_____

OPEN SCENE #5

A: I didn't see that.
B: You didn't.
A: Really
B: I saw it. Sometime ago. Really. Do you like it? Do you? Is that what you want? Because if you do, that's it.
A: I don't know what to say.
B: Yes you do.
A: What should I say?
B: Whatever you like.
A: But I don't know. It's a complete surprise to me. I mean, I've been waiting a long time. I've thought about it for a long time. But I never expected this.
B: Why not?
A: You don't know?
B: This is baffling.
A: Oh no it's not that.
B: Oh that's a relief.
A: It's such a surprise.
B: A pleasant one.
A: Oh thank you.
B: It couldn't be any other way.

_____

1. Where does the scene take place? _____

_____

2. What is the relationship between the characters? _____

_____

_____

_____

_____

3. What is your character's objective? _____

_____

_____

_____

4. What obstacles stand in the way of achieving the objective? _____

_____

_____

_____

5. What, if anything, does your character do to overcome these obstacles?_____

_____

_____

_____

OPEN SCENE #6

A: Go on.
B: What.
A: Go on
B: Well . . . where was I?
A: Where were you? At the river?
B: No, I mean, what was I thinking?
A: I don't know. I don't read minds.
B: Never mind.
A: No. Go on.
B: Go on.
A: Yes. It's important to me. I want to know.
B: I was . . . I mean . . . She was . . . well.
A: Take your time.
B: You know, you're a good friend. I should feel comfortable. . . .
A: But?
B: It's hard to say.
A: Whatever
B: Tomorrow, I promise.

_____

1. Where does the scene take place? _____

_____

2. What is the relationship between the characters? _____

_____

_____

_____

_____

3. What is your character's objective? _____

_____

_____

_____

_____

4. What obstacles stand in the way of achieving the objective? _____

_____

_____

_____

5. What, if anything, does your character do to overcome these obstacles?_____

_____

_____

_____

OPEN SCENE #7

A: Don't move.
B: Why?
A: Don't move, don't move.
B: Why, Why?
A: Oh, I feel ridiculous.
B: You should.
A: Show some feeling would you? I didn't mean that. Ignore it.
B: Yes you did.
A: I can't stand this!
B: So.
A: Look out.
B: What?
A: Wow.
B: What, what?
A: That's it.
B: I don't understand. You've got a strange mind. I don't even know you.
A: Oh yeah?
B: Well.

1. Where does the scene take place? _____

2. What is the relationship between the characters? _____

3. What is your character's objective? _____

4. What obstacles stand in the way of achieving the objective? _____

5. What, if anything, does your character do to overcome these obstacles?_____

OPEN SCENE #8

A: Ah.
B: Yes.
A: How wonderful.
B: Hmm. I hate to break the mood but . . .
A: But what?
B: Maybe I shouldn't say anything. No, I'm sorry it's really thoughtless of me. Go on what were you saying.
A: No, no. I can't. Say what you were going to say
B: Oh gawd! It's nothing, nothing.
A: I can't believe you. I should get used to this.
B: Alright. I'll tell you. (pause)
A: I ran into Joe today.
B: No kidding.
A: Yes, have you seen him?
B: I've decided to leave.
A: (Pause) He seemed to be in exceptionally good spirits. Acted like he had some special secret I should know. What do you mean you're leaving?
B: Sorry.
A: You're always sorry, and it doesn't make any difference. Good-bye.
B: Good-bye.

1. Where does the scene take place? _____

_____

2. What is the relationship between the characters? _____

_____

_____

_____

3. What is your character's objective? _____

_____

_____

4. What obstacles stand in the way of achieving the objective? _____

_____

_____

5. What, if anything, does your character do to overcome these obstacles?_____

_____

_____

_____

OPEN SCENE #9

A: You're late.
B: I know.
A: Watch out.
B: Whew that was close.
A: Really, you are unbelievable.
B: Okay, okay.
A: You'd better do more than say ''okay, okay'' next time.
B: Okay, okay.
A: (Pause) I'm exhausted. I don't think I can keep this up. Where have you been?
B: Never mind. I'm here now. I'll take over.
A: Right. Stay out of my way.
B: What am I here for?
A: Are you serious?
B: No.
A: Good. Say, watch that.
B: Oh, that's incredible!
A: What.
B: I'm getting out of here.

1. Where does the scene take place? _____

2. What is the relationship between the characters? _____

3. What is your character's objective? _____

4. What obstacles stand in the way of achieving the objective? _____

5. What, if anything, does your character do to overcome these obstacles? _____

CHAPTER VI

MOVING ON THE STAGE

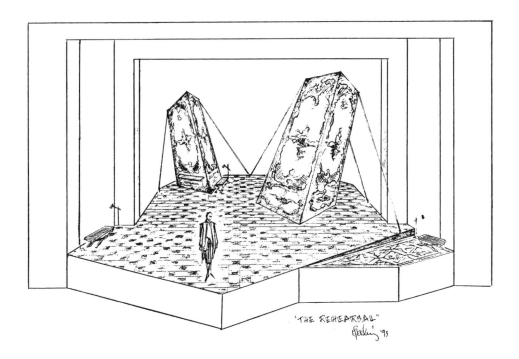

"THE REHEARSAL"
Steeling '93

The actor has the power to transform the performance space into any place, time, or dimension. He achieves this transformation through meaningful use of his voice and body, and clever manipulation of the stage and its devices. But certain physical realities of the stage and their accompanying terminology are essential for the actor to learn in order to succeed in his communication—many of these "tricks of the trade" will be discussed in this chapter.

Stage Configurations

A stage can be defined as any area that is made dramatic by its use as a performance space. Stages can take many forms, from the traditional auditorium style, to more recent, avant-garde spaces that have popped up in such unlikely places as store fronts and warehouses. What follows is the explanation of four basic categories into which most theatrical environments can be placed with top view diagrams.

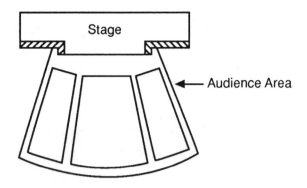

PROSCENIUM—The proscenium, or "picture frame" theatre provides an arch through which the audience views the action on stage. Most commercial theatres are proscenium theatres, in which the audience is clearly separated from the action onstage. The stage setting is often presented in great detail to create a specific reality on stage. The actor, although he generally does not acknowledge the presence of the audience, must be sure that the audience can both see and hear him, despite the fact that the audience is on only one side of the playing area. Many of the terms and concepts that will be explained in this chapter are derived from their use in a proscenium theatre, although they are applicable in other spaces.

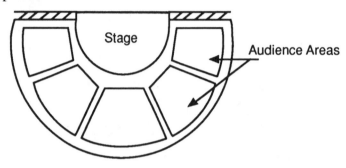

THRUST—The thrust theatre, in which the acting space is quite literally thrust out into the audience, has become quite popular in recent decades. This type of configuration draws the audience closer to the action, and gives the actors a stronger sense of the audience's presence and energy. Scenery is often minimized in this arrangement (only the "back wall" is available for scenic display), so costumes, lighting, and selective **PROPERTIES** (furniture and any objects the actors may handle) must convey more meaning. But the sense of immediacy and involvement that the audience gains will more than make up for any visual elements lost. Although the actor's physical relationship to the audience seems less artificial than in a proscenium theatre, the actor must still be conscious of staying **open** to audience view (this term will be more fully explained in the section titled Stage Position).

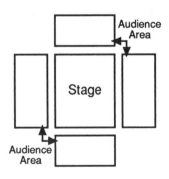

ARENA—The arena theatre is one in which the audience completely surrounds the playing area, and the actors make their entrances through aisles, or through a vomitorium (a tunnel or opening cut into the audience area). The actor's responsibility to stay open is all the more important and one simple rule to follow is to keep your back toward the nearest vomitorium. However unavoidably someone in the audience will often be looking at your back, even if only briefly so you must also learn to be expressive with your back. Scenery is even further reduced, making its specificity all the more valuable. The proximity of audience to actor allows for an intimacy far greater that in the preceding configurations. The acting demands total focus and intricate detail, since the audience members may be three or four feet away.

ENVIRONMENTAL—Environmental theatre spaces often completely disregard the idea of separation of actors and audience. A more traditional theatre space may be restructured, putting spectator seating "on stage" and acting areas in and among seating areas; or a non-traditional space may be employed, such as a park, museum, warehouse, or loft space. Productions in these settings seek a total audience immersion in the theatrical world, and can be particularly effective if that realm is a powerful one, such as an asylum, a war zone, or a factory.

Regardless of the type of acting space in which you are called to perform, and the complexity or simplicity of the visual elements which are provided, it's every actor's responsibility to make the audience believe that the character is present in the actual setting (i.e., a Victorian room, a forest, a suburban home) specified by the playwright.

Stage Directions

The next step in the process of an actor's orientation to a particular stage involves his ability to find his way around, frequently to follow a director's or playwright's instruction. These stage directions give all of the theatre artists a common vocabulary on which to draw for plotting movement, scenic pieces, prop placements, or lighting elements on the stage. For example your teacher or director may give you blocking such as "to cross down right" (in your script you notate this as XDR) and you need to understand these directions as well as you would understand a person telling you to make the next right turn when driving somewhere.

UPSTAGE AND DOWNSTAGE—Downstage is the area of the stage closest to the audience. Upstage is the space furthest from the audience. These terms date from theatres of the fifteenth century, which often had sloped floors to elevate the action at the rear of the stage for better audience viewing. These "raked" floors created a stage environment in which the front edge, or downstage area, was quite literally lower than the back edge, or upstage area. Raked platforms are occasionally incorporated into twentieth century scenic designs, but even in their absence, this terminology remains.

STAGE RIGHT AND STAGE LEFT—These directions are determined by the actor's right or left as he faces down stage. Stage right and stage left, when combined in an instruction with downstage and upstage, further specify the area of the stage. Downstage left means toward the front edge of the stage, and to the actor's left. This illustration shows a top view of the areas.

Back Wall of Stage

UR	UC	UL
DR	DC	DL

Audience Area

ABOVE AND BELOW—The term above is used when an actor crosses upstage of or behind another actor, or piece of scenery or furniture. Similarly, below indicates that an actor crosses downstage of, or in front of his partner or prop.

STRENGTH OF AREAS—When all other factors are equal, the strongest area of the stage is downstage center, followed in order by upstage center, downstage right, downstage left, upstage right, and upstage left.

The center areas are strongest because of the way the proscenuium arch frames them, and the accessibility of their view to all audience members, even in theatres with bad sightlines. The stage right areas are generally speaking stronger than left, since in western culture we read from left to right. Platforms and other scenic devices can be used to strengthen any area, but on a bare stage, the preceding rules will hold.

Groundplans

A groundplan—or floor plan, is a top view map upon which the actor unveils the dramatic action of the play. This drawing, when formulated by a scenic designer in conjunction with a director, is quite detailed, providing information about doors, windows, platforms, steps, fireplaces, furniture and other scenic elements the actor will use. The ground plan does not dictate specific actor movement or blocking, but it does help establish traffic patterns and entrances; and it must suit certain requirements often established in the text of a play integral to the telling of the story.

If you are cast in a given production, frequently you will be given a groundplan generated by the production team months in advance, which you must read and understand. In many types of theatre, rehearsals are not held in the actual performance space, and/or they are held without full scenic elements present for most of the rehearsal period. A stage manager will tape the parameters of the ground plan to the rehearsal floor; and the actors must observe these boundaries.

If you are working on a scene for an acting class, you may be required to formulate your own ground plan for class use. This groundplan will not be fully realized scenically—i.e. platforms, steps, walls, chandeliers, and appropriate furnishings—it must draw upon the elements you are provided in your lab space. You might use free standing flats (light weight stage wall) or folding screens to create walls. But imagination and clever use of a few guidelines can enable you to make use of the space in a dynamic manner.

ENTRANCES—The character who enters or exits usually alters the action on stage, so it follows the area from which he enters should be a dominant one; thus, the upstage center entrance would be strongest. Additonal entrances should be placed with some sense of architectural logic—as they would be in a normal room. One should generally avoid putting all of the entrances on one side of the stage; this move would create traffic pattern problems.

FIREPLACES AND WINDOWS—Fireplaces and windows can be extremely useful in terms of motivating movement on the set if they are properly placed. Putting either of these elements upstage center (along the back wall of the set) would give a fireplace or window prominence in the visual picture, but would make it difficult for an actor to effectively use the area and still remain ''open.'' Placing these elements downstage on a side wall, in areas much closer to the center of the action, allows actors to gravitate towards them and still remain seen.

FURNITURE—People tend naturally to move toward furniture, so its effective placement on stage is essential to a good ground plan. Although one might use the same furniture in a stage setting of a living room as in the real thing, the theatrical groundplan must provide ample room for traffic, easy access to entrances and exits, relationship between different conversational groupings, and motivation for actors to cross from one area to another logically. In a classroom setting, since platforms, step units, windows, or flats (theatrical walls) are generally unavailable, furniture placement constitutes the most important element of ground planning.

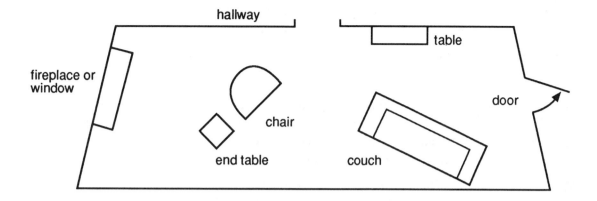

Look at the setting above and analyze its use of the elements discussed in the preceding sections. Although it is simple, it provides actors with:

1. A strong upstage center entrance/exit and a weaker but still useful alternative (stage left).
2. Furniture that is grouped in relationship to the other furniture; the sofa, for example allows actors to lean, sit, recline, or lay. It allows the actor to cross all the way around it (unlike the sofa in a conventional home which is often pushed against a wall), as well as sit on the back of it or stand behind it and still be seen. The chair is far enough away from the sofa to be a separate area, or island. Characters at odds in a scene could each claim a territory on this floorplan, or two characters in agreement could share the space quite easily.
3. The fireplace or window areas are accessible and quite visible, and the upstage right and upstage left areas are available for character isolation or retreat. The downstage center area is free for a romantic picnic, a violent struggle, or other less formal action.

Although an effective ground plan can greatly aid actors, it can't substitute for focused, committed work in a scene, and the actor's endowment of the space. This sort of furniture arrangement is ideal for students with little knowledge of scene design. A particular text may call for an additional element—another door, a dining table, or a window seat—that could easily be substituted for one of the elements shown in the drawing.

Rehearsal furniture is generally intended to be versatile and sturdy, rather than attractive or comfortable. Wherever you work, please treat the space and the objects within it with respect. Don't move furniture in or out of the room, and please clear the stage, or "strike" your furniture when you are finished with it. Learn to act successfully enough that you don't damage furniture. No truly professional, able actor ever destroys furniture. Stop the action of your scene if property or individuals are in danger of being harmed. Control must be taught and learned.

Stage Positions

Previous to the twentieth century, theatrical conventions dictated that actors face downstage at all times. But with the advent of realism and naturalism, actors gained the freedom to use other body positions—in relation to the audience, and each other. Although the actor's face is still an important communication tool, the body can express just as much meaning.

The actor's body when seen in relationship to the audience, can be described in five positions:

FULL FRONT—The actor's body and head face directly downstage.

QUARTER—The actor positions himself facing 45 degrees away from the audience. If he were standing at center stage he would angle his head and body toward down stage left or right areas.

55

PROFILE—An actor faces directly stage right or left with his body turned 90 degrees away from the audience.

THREE QUARTER—An actor faces a point halfway between profile and full back.

FULL BACK—The actor's back is to the audience; he is facing directly upstage.

Generally speaking, the more fully the actor faces the audience, the stronger his position. Each of these positions can, however, be strengthened by use of the head, or standing erect. Sitting, slouching, kneeling, lying down, or turning one's head away from the audience, although it may communicate more interesting dramatic action, generally weakens an actor's position.

All of the discussion of the positions has assumed the presence of one actor. Actors in relationship to each other can shape many moments and can pictorially tell the story before a line of dialogue has ever been spoken. Study the following configurations of two actors in relationship to each other as seen from above.

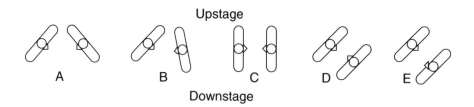

Upstage

Downstage

Figure A shows each actor in QUARTER position—in equal relationship to each other and to the audience. This is the most commonly used position.

Figure B shows a variation on this position, which gives the upstage actor a bit more prominence; it might be used in a scene involving some sort of intimacy or secrecy.

Figure C gives the audience the same view of both actors, plus it places the actors themselves in a more confrontational configuration. This position might be used for arguments or emotional outbursts.

Figure D shows the downstage actor giving his complete head and body focus to the upstage actor. The upstage actor presumably is relating most of the story, with the downstage actor silent or making occasional interjections.

Figure E gives greater prominence to the upstage actor, but allows the audience to see the facial expressions of the downstage actor, thereby increasing his presence and communicative power beyond the amount he had in figure D.

All of these figures have shown the relative power of certain pictures, composed of actors on stage. But most theatre forms are not static—they are a free-flowing and continuous series of stage pictures that continue to tell the story. Whatever your position on stage and your movement across the stage, you must stay open, that is, make an effort to keep your face and front visible to the audience.

Blocking

The planned and lifelike pattern of movements and activities on the stage is called BLOCKING.

The dramatic action of a play can dictate that an actor create on stage a moment he has not lived, and possibly will never live, in his own life—such as fighting in a battle, or commiting a murder. But, more often than not, actors must re-create simple actions—such as getting dressed, talking on the phone, or preparing a meal—in a believable or logical manner. Although much stage movement or acting of this type finds a parallel to real life, its execution on stage must take on new dynamics.

Making Choices with Blocking

Teachers and directors "block" plays and scenes in different ways. More experienced actors are frequently given the opportunity to improvise blocking on the set, to "go with their impulses"; in this situation, the director will eventually step in to make adjustments to increase visibility, solve traffic problems, and heighten the conflict. Some directors give a general pattern to movement ("enter through the SL door, and arrive at the couch by this line, but first explore the setting") but leave room for the actor's interpretive input. Other directors will "pre-block" scenes (devise blocking patterns before the rehearsal time), and give their actors a step-by-step plan. Although this method seems to place restrictions on actors, it is often essential in crowd scenes, where the director must first function as a traffic cop in order to tell the story of the scene in a focused manner. In case of violent or sexually explicit scenes, the director must do careful choreographic work, to insure that the actors are safe and comfortable with blocking.

Good blocking should go beyond creating order on stage, and strong pictorial elements. It must reflect the underlying action of the scene. An audience watching should know at all times who is in control, what spaces they control, who supports them, and who opposes them. The blocking must support the text but also embody what is not expressed verbally.

Many ideas for movement come directly from the text of the play. Stage directions are included in most editions, particularly in the acting editions, (published by a theatrical publisher such as Samuel French, Inc., or Dramatists Play Service), which also include useful information such as prop lists and groundplans. In an acting edition, the stage directions are generally taken from the stage manager's prompt book of the original, or most prominent production of the play. Although sometimes helpful, these notes may be very specific to that particular groundplan, or a certain director's or actor's approach to the text. Actors should consider them a possible interpretation, but not a decisive one. Look for activities in the script that support the action—a phone call that brings an important revelation, a kiss that begins an affair—and disregard other notations that may not make sense out of context.

All types of blocking—whether specified in the script, sculpted by a director, or evolved in rehearsal—must be endowed with meaning by the actor in order to create a believable moment in a character's stage life. Blocking must be motivated—justified, as an action the character takes in order to accomplish main and immediate objectives. If your lines dictate that you are looking out the front door at a certain time ("There's Natalie on the sidewalk"), but give no clear cut reason why you are at the door, then you must invent one. If a director has asked you to remain at the sofa in order to clear the area downstage of it, create an inner justification for your character's presence there.

Often, beginning actors feel uncomfortable making choices that involve strong action. Don't be afraid! Any action or activity that you try in the proper environment (i.e. a work-through rehearsal), can easily be discarded if it is unsuccessful. There are rarely bad or good or "right" choices—just more interesting ones. Start simple; if your scene does not call for extensive movement, then only move when it strengthens your argument, or helps you get closer to your objective. Random movements detract from the life of the scene. And keep in mind that there are hundreds of ways to communicate state of mind in the form of small movements which you can execute simply seated in a chair. Beware of repeated actions, patterns, or gestures. If they are not carefully linked to the action's intention, they will become hollow. A scene may specify that a certain activity is present throughout—such as washing dishes. Let the activity change as the conflict of the scene changes. The way you handle the dishes—obliviously, carefully, violently—will reflect your characters inner state and how it changes moment to moment.

The stage and its use involves technical skills that may seem obtuse at first but once their use becomes second nature, the actor finds creative freedom within these limits, and his work is magnified greatly.

EXPLORING THE SCRIPT

A playwright's inspiration, his collective experience, and his imagination combine to form the text of a play. As actors, we must try to unlock the power and mystery of his message in an active, stimulating manner on stage. This process begins with careful study of the play.

Beginning actors sometimes believe that an analytical approach to a play prevents their own impulses, spontaneity, and creativity from entering the work. They forget that acting involves many conscious, left-brain activities that must be accomplished before the artistic, or right-brain work can happen in a directed or channelled manner. All perceptive play readers have valuable responses when reading plays, but the actor owes it to himself, to the production ensemble, and to the audience to communicate the truthful action of the play, rather than his own pre-conceived feelings about it.

The left hemisphere of the brain is the center for scientific activity—for thinking—whereas the right side is the home of instinct, impulse, or feeling: the place where "doing" or action begins. Acting requires the simultaneous involvement of both sides in a cooperative manner. The more an actor brings in from the left (study and analysis of the play), the more he can draw from it on the right (the creation of a vivid, three-dimensional character). In Chapter 4, The Actor's Basic Skills, the concepts of **ACTION, OBJECTIVE,** and **OBSTACLE** were introduced. In Chapter 5, these terms were applied to the Open Scene texts in order to clearly establish meaning. The purpose of this chapter is to introduce the use of **ACTION, OBJECTIVE,** and **OBSTACLE,** as well as other related terms, when studying fully scripted plays—in order to theatricalize plays in an exciting manner.

Given Circumstances

An actor must begin his study of the character by playing the role of a news reporter or detective—and asking who, what, where, when, how, and why. The answers to many of these questions will provide given circumstances—a thorough background for the character in his situation, the special world of the play. These given circumstances specify the environment (conditions, time, and place), the previous action (that which has transpired between characters before the play begins) and the character's relationship to the preceding information.

Dialogue is the most reliable source for finding given circumstances. On a second or third reading of your script, you may want to underline all dialogue that refers directly or indirectly to past action. Stage directions, as was noted in the previous chapter, are not always the work of the playwright. They may be based on design choices made for an early production of the play, or on choices that a specific actor made when portraying the character. In a good play, important elements of setting and action are written directly into the dialogue. Feel free to cross out unnecessary stage directions, and re-invent the play for yourself within the confines the author has created.

Look for clues in the dialogue that provide you with answers to the following questions. Be as specific and thorough as possible. Makes notes in the areas below, then organize them into a more complete form using the forms at the end of this chapter.

1. When does the play take place? What year, month, day, hour, and minute?

> **Hints:** A general answer—such as "the 1960's"—may get you into big trouble. For instance, it's essential that the first act of *Vanities* by Jack Heifner takes place before the assassination of John F. Kennedy, and that *Kennedy's Children* by Robert Patrick happens well after. Sometimes exact time is an important factor as well—particularly in the plot of a murder mystery. How does time factor into your play?

_____

_____

_____

_____

2. Where does the play take place? What country, state, city, town, neighborhood, street, building, and room? What is the climate like? The weather?

> **Hints:** The plays of Tennessee Williams are very often particularized to the squalor, grandeur, and swelter of the American urban south. Stanley Kowalski, in Williams' play *A Streetcar Named Desire,* might have a great deal more tolerance for his wife's sister Blanche if the three lived in a breezy cottage on the coast of Maine, rather than the heat and claustrophobia of New Orleans in the summer. Noel Coward's characters would get no kick from champagne if they inhabited the less opulent parts of London, Paris, or New York.

_____

_____

_____

_____

3. What objects fill this place? What furniture? What props are part of the direct or implied action of the play?

> **Hints:** If Martha in *Who's Afraid of Virginia Woolf?* by Edward Albee orders George to sit down, where would he sit? A stuffy wingback, a leather sofa, a rough-hewn bench, or a beanbag chair? Do the dialogue and action suggest an empty space or a crowded one? Is the stage filled with homey clutter (as in *Crimes of a Heart* by Beth Henley) or random junk (from *American Buffalo* by David Mamet)? Are the objects important to your character—like Laura's animal collection in *The Glass Menagerie* (also by Tennessee Williams), or merely functional?

_____

_____

_____

_____

4. Who are the other people who inhabit the world of the play? What is your relationship to them?

> **Hints:** Start with the general parameters of your relationship to the other characters—
> i.e. mother/daughter, brother/sister, husband/wife, employer/worker—and then specify.
> There is a world of difference between the loving, mutually accepting brothers of *Death
> of a Salesman* by Arthur Miller and the competitive, warring brothers in *True West* by
> Sam Shepard. The pure, unconditional love between Romeo and Juliet sharply contrasts
> the forces that hold together Eddie and May in *Fool for Love* (also by Sam Shepard).
> Cite specific lines and actions that illustrate the particularity of each relationship in the play.

_____

_____

_____

_____

_____

5. What past events have shaped current circumstances? How and when does the playwright reveal them?

> **Hints:** In *Streetcar*, Blanche's history jeopardizes her chances for successful integration
> into the Kowalski household. But Williams chooses to reveal her indiscretions slowly
> and carefully throughout the play. The slow boil he creates adds to the dramatic build.
> The adulterous relationship between John Proctor and Abigail Williams in *The Crucible*
> by Arthur Miller is over long before the play begins, but it triggers most of the story's
> urgent and fatal consequences. How does the past "act on" the present in the play you
> are considering?

_____

_____

_____

_____

_____

6. What political, historical, social, religious, and socio-economic indicators are present in the script? What is their impact on the action?

> **Hints:** What kind of punch would *Agnes of God* by John Pielmeier have without the struc-
> ture of the Catholic church? Would *The Grapes of Wrath* (adapted from John Steinbeck's
> novel by Frank Galati) retain its poignancy in an upper middle-class suburb? Careful
> evaluation of these factors may involve historical research to flesh out the details of a
> certain society, regime, or age if it is outside the realm of your experience.

_____

_____

_____

_____

Occasionally you will need to fill out certain aspects of the character's background from your own imagination (carefully guided by the confines of the script) or from various research sources. Some dramatists write from their own experience; biographical studies of Eugene O'Neill, Sam Shepard, and Tennessee Williams can give insights into their plays. Other playwrights dramatize actual historical events—*Inherit the Wind* by Jerome Lawrence and Robert E. Lee deals with the Scopes "monkey" trial—or tell the story of an historical figure, such as Joan of Arc; an actor can find much factual and fictive material to supplement his work on this sort of play. The production history of the play, as documented in reviews and criticism, can help an actor identify details that puzzle him. It would be impossible to do too much of this sort of preparation.

Each of these given circumstances must be evaluated as to its importance in your particular character's world; you may find that some areas of exploration are much more fruitful than others. The playwright has carefully shaped these circumstances to make the character's actions seem appropriate within them. You must enter into this special world fully, and concentrate on what your character does within these given circumstances.

Character

Once we discover and clearly delineate objective, and begin to pursue it in each moment, we start to form a character. The only way to create a truly believable illusion, is to believe the illusion completely *yourself,* buying into and personalizing a character's given circumstances, and immediate and longterm needs. Don't feel like you need to rush to create a full-blown character early in the rehearsal process. Experimentation with the character's actions, with the freedom to play, and to fail, will ultimately lead you to more satisfying and innovative results. Try different physical choices, actions, and line readings; see which brings you closest to achieving your objective. Ask your scene partner and your teacher to describe the moments when they found your work to be believable and compelling. If you have done creative preparation as described in this chapter, trust your instincts and have fun!

Stay focused in action and objective, and try to stay clear of cliched or obvious external character adjustments that will detract from the honesty of your work. Adjustments that will help bring you to a more neutral approach to the character, such as better posture or improved diction are fine to begin with. Then as you begin to understand and experience your character's psychology, physical choices should emerge that create a physicality different from your own. But squeaky voices and funny walks are often traps. Externals must directly serve your pursuit of objective. Everything you do, say, wear, and handle on stage should establish, clarify, or further your basic want. Do *everything* that is necessary to achieve your goal—nothing less—or nothing *more*. Extraneous details are the mark of *indicating,* not acting. Don't *show* things about your character: simply *do* what the character *does*. Use the skills you developed in Chapter 4 to develop a full emotional life and spirit for your character. Consider your character's attributes and values, likes and dislikes. Think about your character's thoughts, hopes, dreams, and fears. This type of reflection will help you stay inside the character's world.

Relationships

When an actor tries to force another actor into action or reaction, he will nearly always establish a relationship. The connection that can be formed between two focused actors, in performance or even rehearsal, can be astounding. This give and take is established when an actor focuses his actions and his lines to get what he wants from the other actors. He attempts to stimulate in his partner spontaneous and real responses that will bounce back to him, and charge his own work. This vitality brings the play electrically to life. Consider the other characters when you plan your actions—they either help or hinder you—or do both alternately. Stay flexible and alert to the needs and dynamics of the moment. During rehearsals, encourage your partner to surprise you in safe but provocative ways. For performances, set the general parameters of blocking, force, and tactics you will use, but still find spark, subtlety, and energy in pursuing your objectives. This technique will keep your work spontaneous and honest.

Dramatic Structure

The final element of textual analysis with which you must be acquainted is dramatic structure. When you are travelling on a highway, from point A to point Z, there are several points through which you must pass before arriving at your destination. These "highway exits" take the characters of a play from their beginning—the **INCITING INCIDENT**—through a series of cause and effect events to a **CLI- MAX**, and finally to a **RESOLUTION**. Often the span between the inciting incident and the climax is comprised of dozens of smaller events, revelations, and intrigues that add fire and interest to the story. But unlike highways, which are often flat and linear for long stretches of roadway, plays have many hills and valleys that are essential to their dramatic structure. Each event *builds* on the previous events, creating dramatic tension, and furthering the elements of plot, character, and theme. Plays are structured to maximize their potential for comedy, tension, and pathos. The death scene of *Romeo and Juliet* can't be presented before their meeting or marriage. Not only would the logic of the story be destroyed, but also the impact of their hasty deaths would be greatly lessened.

Beats and Units

Playwrights specify many divisions of dramatic structure. Most plays are broken down into *acts* and *scenes,* which follow sequentially through the course of the action, and build to a dramatic conclusion. Actors and directors further break down scenes into beats and units. The origins of the term "Beat" are disputed. Some claim it is simply a bad translation of the great Russian acting teacher Stanislavski, who spoke of "bits" or pieces of action that comprise drama. On a very basic level, a beat is made up of several lines of dialogue spoken between characters. Perhaps character A and character B are discussing the rainy weather they are experiencing. In the next moment perhaps they discuss a picnic planned for that day, to celebrate the birthday of character C. In a third moment, they ponder the reaction of character C to the postponement or cancellation of the celebration. Each of these moments can be called a **BEAT.** Each is a separate highway point between Point A and Point Z, and separately they build logically and dramatically upon one another to form a larger action, called a **UNIT.** A Unit, like a Scene, and Act before it, has its own complete shape, comprised of a build, a small crisis, and an element of conflict. Unit changes are often delineated by a shift in conversation topic, and can nearly always be found when a character changes his objective, however subtly. Let's go back to our birthday party scenario: perhaps as Unit #1 ends, character A begins Unit #2 by launching into a lengthy discussion of his own problems, in order to get sympathy from Character B. Character A, by changing his objective, has changed the Unit. Character B has *not* changed his objective, but he must follow the course of the action, or else, if the author permits, he can resist, and create conflict. Working through and determining the anatomy of the scene is a painstaking task, but it gives you a much clearer idea of the playwright's intent, and a clearer map to achieving it.

Once again, in reference to our birthday companions, perhaps in Unit #2, Character B listens patiently to Character A's complaints, then eventually humors and finally ignores Character A. Character A slaps Character B (thus beginning Unit #3) which leads to direct confrontation between the characters. Unit #3 ends when Character C enters having overheard the argument. In the ensuing unit, Character C probes for the reason for the outburst, while Characters A and B attempt to disguise any evidence of disagreement. It is essential to think of these events as *cause-and-effect* related: A does to B, B responds and acts on A, A responds, etc. As was stated earlier in the chapter, all of these actions must be considered as *reciprocal*. If a character performs a long speech on stage either to another character, to himself, or the audience, this monologue will also be comprised of beats and units, and will build toward its own inner climax, and the climax of the play.

Scoring the Script

In order to determine the placement of beats and units within your script, please feel free to make pencil marks on a xerox copy of your scene. This process is called scoring the script. Use a pencil also to jot down blocking notes, and thoughts on character in the margin. To delineate the start and finish of a unit, use brackets along the left hand margin of the text, with arrows that show the exact place where the unit changes. In order to show the smaller, more subtle beat changes use a slash mark (/) in the spot where the conversation shifts and/or builds. Use numbers to label your units, starting with unit #1 at the beginning of your scene or monologue. For each unit, decide on the corresponding action verb that best describes what your character does to other characters in order to further the attainment of his objective within that particular unit. Two actors working on the same role in the same scene may come up with slightly different verbs, or slightly different placement of a beat changes: these are the subtleties that distinguish one actor from another. Try to be as specific as possible in the choices you make, and feel free to disregard them and try others if they are not satisfying. By writing everything in your script in pencil, you reserve the right to alter your original choices when frustration leads to inspiration. In order to give yourself ample room for marks and note-taking, you may want to enlarge your script on a photocopy machine and/or glue the xeroxed pages separately into a notebook. A notebook works especially well, since it gives you ample space in which to write any notes or comments you may receive from your instructor or classmates, or to include notes from research materials.

On the next few pages are forms that you can use as formal character analysis sheets for scenes and monologues. You may want to photocopy extra sheets for future use.

The methods of textual analysis detailed in this chapter form a general outline for approaching the script. Your own experiences and world view will bring to this format unique results. There is no ''right'' or ''perfect'' answer or choice, just more or less effective or interesting ones. Find what works best for you.

CHAPTER VIII

MONOLOGUES AND AUDITIONING

A monologue is a long speech or talk given by one person; it may last from forty-five seconds to more than five minutes. Within a play monologues are an integrated part of the action. Your character remains focused on the other characters on the stage and you speak in order to achieve your objective. The only distinction with a monologue is that since it is longer you may have transitions (changes from one action or tactic to another), within the speech; and you must make the changes of thought within your own imagination.

Sometimes the monologue is spoken by the character alone on stage. The character is either speaking directly to the audience with an objective to include them in the action, inviting them in sharing secrets; or the character is working out a conflict within his own thoughts, in soliloquy form. This kind of soliloquy most often appears in Shakespeare's plays.

Auditioning

Monologues of 1 to 3 minutes are often extracted from a play for use as an "audition piece." An audition piece is a well-prepared and polished presentation of monologues. When you do the initial audition to be cast in a play, or to be accepted into an actor-training school, usually you will present two pieces; one of a character very similar to you, and the other a contrasting character that shows something unpredictable or different from you.

Work on a monologue within a scene or play will be just like your work on the rest of the scene. However, preparing a monologue for an audition involves several special elements and much more rehearsal time. You can consider auditioning as a special craft in itself with skills and preparation unique to it. The audition is the actor's job interview, and every actor learns to do it. It's a good idea to learn to *enjoy* it, too.

The unique qualities of a monologue in an audition situation are:

1. You are without the other characters on stage with you; you must fully create the person you are speaking to in your imagination.

2. You must position the imaginary other character you are speaking to on stage or in the audience, so that you are speaking toward the auditioners.

3. You are in an empty space with a chair and sometimes a table, and no set or props.

73

4. You usually have 5 minutes or less to introduce yourself, get to the full emotional, psychological state required for each monologue and deliver it. Unlike in a play or scene, there is no progression of actions or build-up. Snap—you must be there in the reality of the moment of the scene.

5. Your introduction of your real self can be as important as the character portrayal.

If you have found your acting class satisfying and challenging, you may want to take on the larger challenge of being in a play. The information below will help you successfully complete an audition.

Choosing A Piece

Look for a monologue that hits home for you. When you read it you are moved by it, and you say to yourself, "I understand this person. I really know what they feel like, it's just like me."

Look everywhere for the monologue. Feel free to skim through plays: you don't have to read every play through to its end. Look for solid chunks of writing from five to ten or more lines long. If you find something you like, read the scene it is contained within. There are lots of other places to find monologues: novels, short stories, magazines, films. You will also find monologue books in the library which are filled with choices. Once you find a monologue you like, you can find the play and read it.

Choose a monologue that expresses you, and gives the auditors a feeling of being with you intimately, and a feeling that you (the character) are revealing something new. Find a speech that does more than explain something or tell about something. Find a speech that has a build, has energy, suspense, and conflict. Watch out for speeches that are at the climactic point of the play and have extremely high emotions. They are difficult to play, and sometimes hard to watch outside of the context of the play. Your monologue can have elements of surprise, but shy away from foreign accents, graphic language or a shock value. Usually the auditor pays more attention to the shock than to your ability to act. Also, try to stay within your age range. In professional theatre particularly, directors try to cast the right age actor (within 5–10 years) for most roles.

Pick something modern or contemporary in a naturalistic style, especially when you are first starting out. If you are auditioning for a classical play, for example Shakespeare, you may be requested to speak a monologue in verse. This type of piece is more challenging. You should get an expert coach, and make sure you fully understand the text.

If you know what play you are auditioning for try to find a monologue from another play by the same author or another play of the same general style. Do not do a speech from the play you are auditioning for. Your interpretation of the speech may be at direct odds with that of the director.

Often there are time limits set for auditions. Make sure the monologue is slightly shorter than the time you are allotted. If you need to cut out some lines, be sure to preserve the meaning and the logical progressive build. Don't paste a lot of short speeches together to make one longer one. Definitely *do not* use a piece where the other character says something to you in the middle. You should *never* have to pretend you are listening to the other character talk to you!

When you have an opportunity to do two pieces, your second piece can be a bit riskier. This means the character can be different from you, very funny or quirky or unusual. In any case, the second piece should be quite different from the first monologue.

Create a collection of monologues in a folder so you have more than one or two to choose from. Every time you "work up" a monologue, put it in the folder. Eventually you'll have five or six monologues you have prepared, used, and you know work well for you. Sometimes, when you do a particularly successful audition the auditors will ask you if you have anything else prepared. You'll show them another piece and create an even stronger impression.

Preparing the Piece

Once you have found the piece or monologue you are going to use, read the play or story through thoroughly several times.

Then work on the monologue as you would any text. Answer the questions of when, where, who and what to establish the **given circumstances** of the monologue, the scene in which it occurs, and the world of the play. Explore several objectives for the monologue and choose the most **active objective** you can in relationship to the character's main objective within the play. Make the stakes **very** high as if what you need is of life and death importance. As you pursue the objective throughout the monologue, choose strong **actions.** Determine a clear **obstacle** that the character must work against as well as the clearly perceived challenge in getting the other character to listen to you and give you what you need. Also establish your **relationship** with the other character very specifically. Visualize in detail who you are speaking to, and how they are reacting to you. Be certain that image of the other character is there every time you do the piece.

Rehearse in such a way that you cut out any unnecessary pauses (this usually means all pauses). Make your transitions quickly and as you speak. Maintain the pace and energy of the speech to its conclusion.

Make clear physical and vocal character choices but keep them very subtle. Unless you do a second contrasting piece, or you are auditioning for a comedy, a bold characterization will be more off-putting than effective. If you have done specific enough work on given circumstances, the character will emerge.

Finally, make sure that you rehearse with enough vocal volume. Learn to speak with enough vocal energy to fill a large theatre and still feel genuine.

Introducing Yourself

Another very important part of preparing your audition is to rehearse a simple and direct introduction. Practice it along with the monologue to develop a smooth and quick transition from speaking in a friendly, warm manner as yourself, to speaking as the character.

As yourself, your objective should be something like "to share," "to welcome;" your inner dialogue may be something like "we'll have a great time working together," "I love working as an actor and I'm easy to work with; here's the piece I'm most excited about doing right now." Your text will run something like "Hi," or "Hello" or "Good morning," "My name is (whatever it is, of course)," "I'll be playing Blanche from *A Streetcar Named Desire* by Tennessee Williams." (In other words the name of the character, the play and the playwright.) If the stage manager announces your name as you go up, you will not need to say your name. Try to find this out before hand. You will **never** need to explain the story or what is happening at that point in the play. That will be obvious if you do a successful presentation.

Getting Feedback

Once you are thoroughly prepared, find someone you trust, and who is experienced in theatre to coach you. They should give you feedback on whether or not your objective is clear and urgent enough, as well as tell you what moments are working particularly well. You can ask them about blocking or certain moments you are not sure about. They can help you polish your pieces.

Next, perform your pieces everywhere and anywhere for friends and even family. Get used to performing them in different spaces—small rooms, large theatres, classrooms—and get comfortable performing for lots of people. Your audience doesn't need to be expert thespians at this stage. All they need to be able to tell you is whether it is interesting and believeable, and easily heard, seen, and understood. You'll be able to tell for yourself if it is well-prepared, solidly learned, and effective.

It is advisable to always have a monologue in performance shape. Once you have found a piece that works well for you, use it over and over. It can be effective to work up a piece and then not audition with it for several months. Every couple of weeks review the lines and try it out again. When you come back to it to brush it up for an audition, you will be working with something with which you are familiar. Remembering the lines will be a breeze. You will also have the added benefit of finding new insights into the character and the speech. Keep the monologue fresh by trying out new images or different details in given circumstances. Be sensitive to impulses to do new actions when you are rehearsing old pieces for a new audition. This way you will avoid becoming mechanical or automatic in your performance.

At the Audition

Arrive at the audition site at least one-half hour early. Be ready to audition the moment you get there. Sometimes other actors have not shown up for their time, and you may be asked to go in early. You should warm-up before you leave home; you may not have adequate space to do so at the site. Use some of the body and voice warm-ups presented in Chapter IV that leave you feeling relaxed, focused and energized.

Arrive at the audition site looking good. Don't wear your junky jeans and your ratty T-shirt. Also, don't wear a suit and tie or cocktail dress or other outfits that restrict your movement. Wear something that makes **you feel** great, makes you feel comfortable, and that you can move in. With some imagination you can even select an outfit that is something like the character. If a woman wears high heels and her character is more athletic or barefoot, she can slip them off on stage as she begins the monologue. Don't bring or use any extraneous items (or individuals).

Be congenial with the stage manager and other assistants who will check you in for the audition. Be friendly and convivial with other actors, but be sensitive to actors wanting to focus on preparing for their audition. Be quiet and cooperative. Find ways to keep yourself relaxed and focused. If there are any details of which you are unsure (like where to enter and if they are announcing your name or not), feel free to ask the stage manager.

After the Audition

Once you have finished, be sure to find out when the director will be casting the show, and if callbacks are involved. Callbacks are generally readings from the script that occur on another day. Also make sure you know if they will be calling the cast members, or if they will be posting a cast list instead. If they post a list be sure you know where and when it will be posted. Then wait to be notified. Don't pester the stage manager or director with unnecessary calls.

Before you find out how the casting goes, evaluate your own audition. Consider how well focused on the reality of the play you were, and how strongly you pursued your objective. Evaluate how comfortable you felt, and if your introduction was direct and friendly. You know how you did, and you can learn from any mistakes you made. Don't use the fact of whether or not you were cast to tell you if you did an effective audition or not. There are many more elements a director considers than just your ability to act. It's even possible for an actor to do the best audition there and not be cast because he was too short or tall, or he didn't fit the director's image of the character, or many other reasons.

If you find you were not cast in the play, you can try to arrange to talk to the director about what did or didn't work about your audition. This sort of feedback can be helpful if the director is open to providing it.

If you want to be in a play, keep auditioning, and continue getting coaching. BREAK A LEG!

CHAPTER IX

REHEARSAL TECHNIQUES

When producing a play, the actors and directors spend from two to eight weeks rehearsing the play. On average that constitutes between 90 and 200 hours of rehearsal time, or 1 to 2 hours per minute of performance time. This formula is good to use in planning how much rehearsing you should do to prepare your scene for class; a two minute scene should get at least two hours work, a ten minute scene ten hours work. Since you're just starting out, planning more time than this would be wise: certainly don't plan less. You will also need to spend time outside of your scheduled rehearsal time memorizing your lines, and reading and making notes on the play and your character. Be sure to allow sufficient time to accomplish all of the above each week of your academic schedule. It is never a good practice to leave everything to the last minute, i.e. cramming for a test, doing an ''all nighter'' on a paper. It absolutely will not work in an acting class because your teacher will be working very directly with you—if you are unprepared, any personal coaching they may provide will be a waste of everyone's time. On the other hand, if you have rehearsed and prepared fully, you'll be amazed at how much more you discover working on the scene in class, and your progress toward becoming a successful actor will speed ahead.

To make your rehearsals most useful, follow the guidelines below.

Rehearsal Guidelines

1. Be prompt! Consider any time you have reserved with your partner and/or instructor as sacred. Even in the busiest of times, their schedules are probably just as hectic as yours. Be sure that you have the phone numbers you may need, however, if an emergency comes up.

2. Be prepared! If you are supposed to have your lines memorized on a given day, make sure this work is thoroughly completed. Bring any props or costume pieces that are necessary for use in the scene. Wear clothing that is conducive to rehearsal.

3. Be respectful! Treat your partner's time, body, spirit, and personal boundaries with the utmost respect. In turn, if your partner behaves inappropriately in rehearsal, do not hesitate to discreetly inform your instructor.

4. Select a location that is suitable for rehearsal. If you are enrolled in a university, ask your teacher if there are rehearsal spaces available to you on an hourly sign-out basis. Perhaps there is an empty lounge in your dormitory that would be useful. If you must rehearse in a dorm room or apartment, try to make this space as free of distraction as possible. Turn off stereos, radios and television. Encourage roommates to clear out during your rehearsal time.

5. Devise a warm-up that works for you and your partner. This procedure may be slightly different each time you rehearse. But it is essential to bring your body and mind to the state necessary to do productive acting work. You may select physical and vocal warm-ups described in this text, or presented by your instructor in class. Or you may use theatre games such as mirroring or improvisations to get your creativity re-activated.

A few additional courtesies:

1. If you have used a classroom or rehearsal room to rehearse in, leave the room cleaner than when you entered it. Replace any furniture you used against the walls so the space is clear and neat. Throw away any trash—paper, cups, drink cans, etc.—that you brought in with you.

2. Always be sure that the physical choices you make and the impulses you follow are in no way harmful to your partner, your audience, yourself or your surroundings. Feel free to be inventive with furniture but don't be abusive. If a chair breaks or anything is damaged it is clear you are out of control: there is no excuse for it.

3. Don't tell your acting partner how he should play a scene. There is no one way to play a character. Be open and responsive to whatever he has his character do. You will discover many things in the scene you won't think of yourself.

You can work *with* your partner to plan out some blocking after you've rehearsed for a while. Also if your partner is confused about or having difficulty with a specific line or moment and he *asks your* opinion then you might make some suggestions. Still, rather than giving line readings, discuss your ideas about the play, and the other actor will get some new ideas for his own character.

Creative Rehearsal Challenges

Exercise 1: Keep Things Fresh!

Going through the same lines and blocking with drill-sergeant precision will dull your creative response to the material. Find ways to liven things up. Pursue different courses to fulfill your objective. In rehearsals, feel free to try new things and surprise your partner. As you get closer to your final performance of your scene you will want to set the gestures and vocal choices of your character as well as the blocking. However, you will only come up with the most interesting choices by experimenting with many different possibilities in the beginning. Be playful and impulsive. Turning away from your partner at a pivotal moment, or removing an imaginary hair from his or her shoulder will keep the scene fresh, and stimulate your partner to creatively challenge you.

Exercise 2: Filling in the Life

Place your characters in another scene, either one earlier in the play that you can actually read in the script, or one that you devise. If you are playing Blanche in *A Streetcar Named Desire,* in the climactic scene with Stanley, it will be helpful to read through and play with the earlier scenes between these two characters that lead up to this confrontation. If you are doing a scene between Blanche and Stella you may want to improvise a scene from their childhood. This scene could be a normal occasion, such as playing in the fields of Belle Reve, or a more somber event, such as the funeral of a parent. You may find your play has important scenes between characters happening *offstage*—i.e. described to the audience, rather than actually shown. This type of scene will be helpful to create improvisationally in rehearsal. Also—consider the moment before the scene begins. Perhaps the author has raised the curtain in the middle of a confrontation. Or maybe your character has just had a painful experience offstage that colors his involvement in the scene under consideration. Explore all of these moments—they will add history and fire to your scene. Of course, be sure to have read the play *several* times before you start.

Exercise 3: A Change of Scenery

Your usual rehearsal space should closely reflect the room in which you'll give the final presentation of your scene. But for the sake of adventure and exploration, try alternative rehearsal spaces. If your scene takes place in a public park, or diner, or train station, and you have access to such a location, spend an hour or two working on your scene in the actual place. This type of work is probably most fruitful when lines are memorized. You may need to adjust or even temporarily discard blocking, but you will find your sensory awareness in terms of place greatly increased. Try to memorize the details of place—color of the sky, temperature of the breeze, smell in the air, hardness of a bench—and recreate these elements in a classroom setting.

Exercise 4: Conditioning Forces and Circumstances

If your scene is a heated debate, and you find yourself shouting all the time, then rehearse in a location where shouting is prohibited. Try your scene in your school library. You'll find that body language, facial expressions, and emphatic tone will give you the greater range that shouting limited. If you need to convince your partner of something in the context of the scene, place a physical obstacle between the two of you: stand on opposite sides of a four-lane road and run the scene. You'll find commercial trucks are terrific obstacles. If your character is clearly the weaker and less powerful in a scene, and you are having trouble bringing across this distinction, have your partner stick his head out of a second or third story window, while you stand on the ground below: run your scene in this configuration. This exercise will give you a stronger sense of your character's powerlessness. Devise other exercises of this sort to flesh out relationships and moments. Here's a list of some other possibilities: playing age, sitting back to back, one character pushing the other, playing blind man's bluff, speaking gibberish, lying down, or jogging. Generally exercises of this sort do not show up in actual theatre performances, except perhaps in the case of Deconstructivist or Absurdist productions, but they are immensely helpful to open-minded actors.

Exercise 5: Physicalize the Struggle of the Scene

If two characters are fighting over a piece of property, try actually grappling with a safe unbreakable object. Or try a tug-of-war with a rope. Sometimes the physical strength of one or the other partner may allow a certain *actor* to win the exercise even if their *character* is less successful in the play. Give this actor a handicap—such as a blindfold, or a full glass of water to carry that he must not spill. This will even things up.

Exercise 6: Increase Vocal and Sensory Awareness

Rehearse in the dark, or with a curtain separation, or over the phone. Very often actors get so accustomed to the lines of the scene that they stop *hearing* and responding spontaneously to them. These exercises, in which your sight is eliminated, will encourage you to really listen to what your partner is saying, and to use your voice in an effective manner to achieve your objective in relationship to them. You may even want to cross out your partner's lines in your script, except for the last few words that give you your cue, in order to avoid shutting off your ears to your partner's message.

Exercise 7: Switch Roles

This exercise can break things up for you in rehearsal, and be fun as a diversion; but it can also give you insights into the other character, and ways in which your character may more completely effect them.

A Special Note about Monologues

A monologue has unique circumstances for rehearsal, since you don't need a partner or a particular setting to successfully rehearse it. You will, however, need *motivation*. In rehearsal, as in performance, you will be alone, and only have yourself to create the spark necessary for lively work. Many of the techniques detailed here can also be useful in rehearsing a monologue. Successful work on a monologue could give you the most useful "product" you get from this course, since you can use this monologue at auditions in the future.

Finally, ask for **Response**. If you have specific questions about how certain elements or moments in your scene are coming across, or will "read" (appear) to your audience, then ask a knowledgeable person to watch your rehearsal and respond. Make sure this person knows what to watch for. Prep them by saying what your concerns are. Ask them to respond by saying what they *saw* in the scene, rather than their opinion or how they would do it themselves. For example, what type of world did you create for them? Were any elements of the scene inconsistent with that world? This type of help is particularly useful when working on a monologue, in which case you don't have even the response of your partner within the scene to gage your effectiveness.

All of these tools, plus others your instructors will provide, and many you will devise on your own, will help make rehearsal a rich and fruitful discovery ground for your acting work.

RESPONDING TO PERFORMANCES AND PLAYS

The final product of the actor's journey is the public performance. While your participation in Introduction to Performance may not lead you to become a professional performer, it will at least have sharpened your perceptions of what makes for a successful, entertaining evening of theatre.

Everything you see from the moment you step into the theatre has been designed to influence your experience of the performance that you view. First, the style of the theatre affects the way in which you experience the play. In Chapter VI the basic differences in stage configurations are discussed. When you walk into the theatre take notice of how the space of the theatre affects you. Then notice the set—the picture that the director and set designer intend for you to see as you wait for the show to begin. Whether it's a drawn curtain or a dimly lit stage setting, how is your mood set for watching the play? Once the production has begun, a myriad of theatrical elements create the world of the play and the way in which you experience it. Lights, music and sound, costumes, props, grouping of actors, and actors' physical and vocal behavior all create the story as the director intends you to experience it. The director may even have written director's notes in the program to influence your reception of his/her concept. With the final bows, the successful performance will leave you with a distinct mood and image. You should walk away having gained some insight into humanity, having questioned some assumptions, or having had your spirits lifted.

As part of your study of acting it is useful to focus your observation on specific aspects of a play and its presentation. By attempting to evaluate the distinct elements of production you become more discerning and appreciative of the theatre.

On the following pages are several forms with questions about shows you have viewed. Take time to answer the questions in detail. Write as if the reader has not seen the play, nor read the script.

Reading Plays

Another way to familiarize yourself with the art of theatre is to read plays. As you gain experience in creating characters, rehearsing exercises and scenes and presenting them, you increase your ability to visualize and interpret the plays that you read. On the next five pages are forms to fill out after reading a play. For each play that you read, fill out one form.

CHAPTER XI

SELF EVALUATION

Self Evaluation Guide—Introduction to Performance

Your Name _____

Your Character's Name _____

Play Title _____

Please discuss your perceptions with regard to each of the following areas, as it applies to the project you have just completed. Please share both your successes and your challenges.

Choice of Material:

Organization/Scheduling:

Groundplanning:

Use of Rehearsal Time:

Communication with Scene Partner:

Script Analysis:

Blocking and Other Physical Choices:

Vocal Choices:

Emotional Connections:

Rehearsal Problems:

Your feelings about the Performance—Before, During, and After:

Feedback from Your Instructor and Classmates:

Other Comments about this Project:

Please reflect upon these statements based on your growth over the entire semester. Feel free to use the back of this page for additional writing.

The most surprising aspect of this course, to me, was:

The most challenging aspect of this course, to me, was:

The most important thing I learned about the craft of Acting is:

The project or exercise that I learned the most from was: (include reasons)

I discovered and/or developed new skills, freedom, creativity, and confidence in these areas:

These skills will help me in my career and my life in the following ways:

In the beginning of the term, the prospect of performing with or for my classmates made me feel:

Now, this prospect makes me feel:

APPENDIX

Conclusion

As you come to the end of your work in Introduction to Performance you will have explored the fundamentals of the craft of acting. It is certain that when you see the next theatrical production you will have a greater appreciation for what the actors on the stage have accomplished. If you are interested in pursuing a career or avocation in performing for the theatre you will need to follow a more concentrated course of study in the skills that are touched on here.

Terms to Know

Endow
Conditioning Forces
Emotional Recall
Trigger Object
Action
Main Objective
Immediate Objectives
Obstacle
Subtext
Proscenium
Thrust
Arena
Properties
Open
Environmental
Up Stage
Down stage
Scenery
Stage Left
Stage Right
Ground plan
Full Front
Quarter
Profile
Three Quarter
Full Back
Blocking
Given Circumstances
Indicating
Inciting Incident
Climax
Resolution
Beats
Units
Scoring
Break A Leg

Possible Titles for Scene and Monologue Use

Titles	Authors	Codes
Cloud 9	Caryl Churchill	m f fm
Top Girls		f ff
Tracers	John DiFusco	m mm
The Marriage of Betty & Boo	Christopher Durang	F m fm
Baby with the Bathwater		f m fm ff
Beyond Therapy		fm f m
The House of Blue Leaves	John Guare	f m
Landscape of the Body		f m fm
The Diary of Anne Frank	Albert Hackett	f fm
Plenty	David Hare	f m fm ff
Vanities	Jack Heifner	f ff
Crimes of the Heart	Beth Henley	f ff fm
The Miss Firecracker Contest		f ff fm
As Is	William Hoffman	m mm
Painting Churches	Tina Howe	f
The Art of Dining		f fm
Coastal Disturbances		f fm ff
Gemini	Albert Innaurato	m f ff fm
Orphans	Lyle Kessler	m mm
Table Settings	James Lapine	fm f m
American Buffalo	David Mamet	m mm
Sexual Peversity in Chicago		ff mm fm f
Glengarry Glen Ross		m mm
Still Life	Emily Mann	f m fm
Talking With . . .	Jane Martin	f
The Woolgatherer	Wm. Mastrosimone	f m fm
Extremities		f fm
Lone Star	James McClure	m mm
Children of a Lesser God	Mark Medoff	m
When You comin' back Red Ryder?		f m
A Coupla White Chicks . . .	John Ford Noonan	f ff
'Night, Mother	Marsha Norman	f ff
Getting Out		f ff fm
Kennedy's Children	Robert Patrick	f m
Agnes of God	John Pielmeier	f ff
Betrayal	Harold Pinter	fm mm
Hurlyburly	David Rabe	f m fm
Album	David Rimmer	f ff m mm fm
Educating Rita	Willy Russell	f fm
A Lie of the Mind	Sam Shepard	f m fm ff mm
Curse of the Starving Class		f
Motel Chronicles		m
True West		m mm

Play	Author	Codes
Cowboy Mouth		f fm
A . . . My Name is Alice	Joan Silver	f
The Real Thing	Tom Stoppard	f m fm
Nuts	Tom Torpor	f
Key Exchange	Kevin Wade	f m fm
Uncommon Women and Others	Wendy Wasserstein	f ff
Isn't It Romantic		f ff fm
The Heidi Chronicles		f ff fm
Loose Ends	Michael Weller	m f fm
Moonchildren		fm m f ff mm
Talley's Folly	Lanford Wilson	f m fm
The Effect of Gamma Rays on Man-in-the-moon Marigolds	Paul Zindel	f ff

Explanation of the codes:

f	=	Female monologues
m	=	Male monologues
ff	=	Scenes between women
mm	=	Scenes between men
fm	=	Scenes between women and men

Books For Further Study

Adler, Stella. *The Technique of Acting.* New York: Bantam Books, 1975.

Ball, David. *Backwards & Forwards: A Technical Manual for Reading Plays.* Carbondale: Southern Illinois University Press, 1983.

Barker, Sarah. *The Alexander Technique.* New York: Bantam Books, 1990.

Barton, Robert. *Acting on Stage and Off.* New York: Holt, Rinehart and Winston, 1989.

Benedetti, Robert. *The Actor at Work.* Englewood Cliffs, N.J.: Prentice Hall, 1990.

Brebner, Ann. *Setting Free the Actor: Overcoming Creative Blocks.* San Francisco: Mercury House, 1990.

Brockett, Oscar G. *The Theatre: An Introduction* (4th ed.). New York: Holt, Rinehart & Winston, 1979.

Brook, Peter. *The Empty Space.* New York: Atheneum, 1984.

Cohen, Robert. *Acting One.* Palo Alto: Mayfield Publishing Company, 1984.

Cohen, Robert. *Acting Power.* Palo Alto: Mayfield Publishing Company, 1978.

Cole, Toby, ed. *Acting: A Handbook of the Stanislavski Method.* New York: Crown Publishers, 1971.

Cole, Toby and Helen Chinoy, eds. *Actors on Acting.* New York: Crown Publishers, 1970.

Corson, Richard. *Stage Makeup.* New York: Appleton-Century-Crofts, Inc., 1988.

Felner, Mira. *Free to Act: An Integrated Approach to Acting.* Fort Worth: Holt, Rinehart, and Winston, Inc., 1990.

Hagen, Uta. *Respect for Acting.* New York: Macmillan, 1973.

Harrop, John, and Epstein, Sabin R. *Acting With Style.* Englewood Cliffs, N.J.: Prentice-Hall, 1982.

Hodge, Francis. *Play Directing: Analysis, Communication, and Style.* Englewood Cliffs, N.J., 1988.

Johnstone, Keith. *Impro: Improvisation and the Theatre.* New York: Theatre Arts Books, 1983.

Linklater, Kristin. *Freeing the Natural Voice.* New York: Drama Book Publishers, 1976.

Martinez, J. D. *Combat Mime: A Non-Violent Approach to Stage Violence.* Chicago: Nelson-Hall. 1982.

Shurtleff, Michael. *Audition: Everything an Actor Needs to Know to Get the Part.* New York: Walker, 1978.

Spolin, Viola. *Improvisation for the Theater.* Evanston: Northwestern University Press, 1970.

Spolin, Viola. *Theatre Games for Rehearsal.* Evanston: Northwestern University Press, 1984.

Stanislavski, Constantin. *An Actor Prepares.* Translated by Elizabeth Reynolds Hapgood. New York: Theatre Arts Books, 1936.

Stanislavski, Constantin. *Building A Character.* Translated by Elizabeth Reynolds Hapgood. New York: Theatre Arts Books, 1977.

Organizations for Developing Professionals

Theatre Communications Group (New York City, N.Y.)
University/Resident Theatre Association (New York City, N.Y.)
American College Theatre Festival (Washington, D.C.)